Dan Bongino

Biography

From Top-Ranked Secret Service Agent to Political Firebrand

CONTENT

Chapter 1: Early Years

Chapter 2: NYPD Blue

Chapter 3: In the Line of Fire

Chapter 4: The End of the Clinton Era

Chapter 5: 9/11

Chapter 6: An Assassin Among Us

Chapter 7: Training the Next Generation

Chapter 8: Dignitary Protection and the Fight to Protect

Chapter 9: The "Big Show": The Presidential Protective Division

Chapter 10: Transportation: It's Not Simply about Motorcades

Chapter 11: The President's Life in My Hands

Chapter 12: Missile Treaties and the Return to Indonesia

Chapter 13: Oil Spills, Indonesia Again, and Making a War Zone "Safe"

Chapter 14: Media Spin vs. Security Reality

Chapter 15: Giving Back the Gun and Shield

Chapter 16: From Behind the Camera to the Front

Chapter 17: Israel and a Surprise Entrance into the Primary

Chapter 18: The Campaign Heats Up

Chapter 19: A Political Loss, and Why Action Matters

Chapter 20: The Real Scandal of "Fast and Furious"

Chapter 21: Benghazi: Who Gave the Order to Stand Down?

Chapter 22: Boston: Too Many Agencies, Not Enough Communication

Chapter 23: Our Government Has Failed Us

Chapter 1: EARLY YEARS

Growing up on Rose Lane in Smithtown, New York, with my mother, Judy, father, John, and two brothers, Jim and Joseph, was quiet, calm, and relatively unremarkable for all the right reasons. Each morning, we walked the short distance to Forest Brook Elementary School, which was at the end of our street. My father was a building inspector and licensed plumber, while my mother worked in a supermarket. They allowed a comfortable, quiet existence. All of this was about to change for us, and when it did, it happened quickly, with little indication of what our future held.

My parents were very excellent at covering the problems in their marriage. They rarely argued openly, so to an eight-year-old, everything seemed normal. Their marriage began to deteriorate in the early 1980s, and by 1983, it was a marriage in name only. When I turned nine, I understood what was going on. I recall a disagreement that culminated in a bottle of Fox's U-Bet chocolate syrup shattering on the front porch, leaving a large, dark stain. The memory remains crisp and vivid to this day. With their divorce proceeding, my mother could no longer afford our Smithtown home and opted to relocate to Queens, New York. She was reared in Queens, and while she may have been used to the hardships of city life, my brothers and I were not.

The new Queens apartment was on Myrtle Avenue, above the bar that my grandfather owned. My mother had little money, and the nasty divorce processes dragged on, so her wage from working in the store across the street was our sole source of income. Since my grandfather's death several years ago, the pub has seen few patrons. My mother and her three sisters attempted to handle it with limited success, and living above it was difficult. In addition to the jukebox noise every night, the apartment was small, overcrowded, and rodent-infested. Myrtle Avenue was always congested with cars and individuals in no hurry to contribute to the night's silence.

My mother began seeing a man she knew from her childhood not long after returning to her old area. Mike, or as she called him, "Big Mike," was a grizzled dock worker and former boxer. He was physically imposing, six feet, five inches tall and weighing about 280 pounds. His behavior was considerably different from that of the father we had left behind in Smithtown, and adjusting to his increased presence in the little apartment was tough for my brothers and me.

Mike was a fine man in general, but when he drank, he transformed into someone else totally. He grew up on the rough city streets, where fighting was the norm rather than the exception. Having known nothing but tranquility throughout my childhood, hearing about violence and fighting began to disturb me. After a year at the apartment, Mike moved in with us and became a permanent fixture in our lives. At the time, I was unaware of the ramifications of crossing Mike, but I rapidly discovered our relationship's boundaries. Sitting in the kitchen one night, Big Mike asked me, in front of my mother, whether I wanted to go to the Ridgewood Grove Arena to watch WWF wrestling. I said half-jokingly, "I have other things to do." These words would come back to haunt me the next morning, when he raged at me for being rude while I lay in bed. I was stunned and terrified, and I resolved never to speak to him again in any way that could be regarded as unfriendly. This was only a hint of what was to come.

A few weeks later, I awoke in the middle of the night to muffled screaming. I closed my eyes, thinking I was having a nightmare, but the noises would not stop. My six-year-old brother Joseph made the mistake of crossing Mike earlier that day, which most sensible people would blame on childhood immaturity. Mike had been drinking and determined that Joseph would be the outlet for his fury. This was the moment our lives changed forever. There are no buybacks for children who swap their youthful innocence for the cruel truth and harsh edges of life. The assault had become a regular ritual for me. Joseph and I never discussed it. Nobody did. We all pretended it never happened, and the rest of the world was content to accept it. With no money, ripped clothes, an empty refrigerator, and an apartment that seemed like a jail, I turned to comic books as an escape. I studied everything I could get my hands on and had dreams only a youngster could have, dreams of superhuman power and the ability to stand up to Mike without fear. The superpowers never materialized, and the harm to my youth was irreversible.

After years of this excruciating repetition, my grandmother offered my mother money to buy a little house just up the street in Liberty Park, Queens. Although it was only a short walk from the flat to the bar, it was far from ideal for rearing a child. My mother's relationship with Mike was now on and off, and she began working for Con Edison, a New York electrical company, where she received a higher salary. Some of our life' harshest edges began to soften, but Mike's edge remained as sharp as ever. After a night of drinking, he made it to our house and started beating on the windows. The constant banging worried me and my brothers. We readied ourselves for the consequences if the window broke and he got hold of us. Mike's sole apparent dread was the cops, so I dialed 911 and timed the seconds until they arrived. I recall seeing them at our front door after they told Mike to leave and realizing right then that I wanted to be one of them. I intended to repay the favor by bringing serenity into the lives of a small child.

Chapter 2: NYPD BLUE

EARLY CHILDHOOD EXPERIENCES ingrained in me a strong determination to never be physically intimidated again, and to do everything within my power to prevent it from happening to others. Law enforcement became a desire of mine, and after two years of college, I began looking into opportunities in federal, state, and municipal law enforcement. After making several calls to the FBI, DEA, US Marshals, and Secret Service, I realized that I would face stiff competition for the limited number of entry-level positions available, and that transitioning from college to a law-enforcement position with one of these agencies would be difficult, if not impossible. I began to evaluate several options and, after careful analysis, decided on the New York City Police Department as the ideal institution to gain both the expertise and contacts required to advance into federal law enforcement. I chose the NYPD cadet program as the most reasonable option, and my father was anxious to assist.

My father had always wanted to work in law enforcement, but a severe case of spinal scoliosis prevented him from pursuing that dream. The cadet program was essentially a paid internship program. It allowed me to attend college full-time while working part-time for the department in a support role, with a contract that required me to serve as a police officer for two years after graduation. The program was an endeavor by the NYPD to recruit more college graduates into its ranks, and it quickly attracted a large number of competent applicants.

At the same time, I was thinking about joining the military and contacted a recruiter for the United States Marine Corps. Staff Sergeant Williams and I had several chats, and my desire to serve our country was strong. My uncle, Gregory Ambrose, was killed in action in Vietnam. My mother never recovered from grief. I knew she'd be scarred by my decision to join the military, but the call was loud and strong. I recall going to my high school's job fair and witnessing the

Marine Corps presentation, where I was captivated by the presiding Marine's valor from every pore.

Despite the gravitational pull of military service on me, I was unable to satisfy my ambition to serve, a decision I would regret for many years. I received a phone call months after submitting my application to the NYPD informing me that I had successfully finished the difficult application process for the cadet program and would have to report for duty in the spring of 1995. At the time, I was living alone and struggling financially. I moved out of my house shortly after my eighteenth birthday due to a physical incident with Mike, and I was working and attending college while figuring out my future. Financial demands weighed on me every day, and I knew that if I accepted the cadet post, military duty would be out of the question, but it would provide me with some financial security and a road forward. I accepted the employment because of my desire to work in law enforcement and to escape the constant financial pressures. My mother cried with relief as I told her the news, and the prospect of losing another member of her family faded.

I was thrilled to join the NYPD cadet program. It was my first real work with mature responsibilities, and I felt privileged to be a part of the program. Although the work demanded maturity, I was still a city lad with a rough edge who was unaccustomed with the formality of a militaristic setting. The cadet training program was a mini-police academy led by officers with extensive military experience. The paramilitary atmosphere began on the first day—when I reported for duty at a local college auditorium, I had just gotten it to the queue to enter the building when a grizzled NYPD veteran yelled, "Get in line, and shut your mouths!" That was all I needed to hear to completely understand how my life was going to alter.

After graduating from the cadet training program and being familiar with military marching, the law, and, most significantly, law-enforcement culture, I was sent to the 114th Precinct in Astoria,

Queens. After an uneasy few days of roaming aimlessly around the precinct, waiting for my duty to end, precinct superiors asked if I might help "upstairs." The second floor of the 114th Precinct was dubbed "the borough," or the command headquarters for the entire borough of Queens. The senior NYPD brass from Queens worked upstairs alongside the staff they brought in from several precincts throughout the city. It was no place for a cadet, the department's lowest-ranking uniformed member, and I didn't get off to a good start. On my first full day in the borough, I was assigned to an afternoon shift after finishing my college classes. When I arrived, I properly noted in the log that I was starting my shift. Ten minutes later, I discovered that I had done the terrible sin of checking in at the exact time I had arrived, "blocked out" a chief who arrived late and was now required to sign in at her actual (late) arrival time. I didn't get off to a good start, but after serving a penance of performing menial duties and being publicly humiliated by the municipal workers, I was forgiven.

Given my youthful appearance, it wasn't long before an affable sergeant who had taken a fancy to me asked if I wanted to conduct covert work. Sergeant Schwach asked me to report to the 111th Precinct in Bayside, Queens, to accompany a team on alcohol enforcement activities. I wasn't a police officer yet and didn't carry a firearm, but the assignment seemed harmless enough. Bayside was a popular middle-class Queens area with a thriving bar scene (where I eventually met my wife). The bars provided economic activity to the area, but also increased crime and trouble from young drinkers and reckless clientele. Some local delis and convenience stores exacerbated the problem by selling alcohol to underage consumers. My mission was to accompany a small group of police officers and a sergeant as they attempted to obtain alcohol from businesses and pubs. The short ride to the first bar on the Long Island Expressway service lane was an exercise in emotional denial. I didn't want the officers to know how frightened I was, so I made small conversation as we drove over to the Pull-Box.

The Pull-Box was a neighborhood tavern owned by a former New York firefighter (which, as I subsequently discovered, influenced the choice to include it in the undercover operation). I stepped into the bar, faking bravery, and sat down among a gathering of fewer than five patrons, which only drew attention to my embarrassing entrance, before ordering a beer. When the bartender asked for my ID, I said I didn't have one, so he asked me to leave. I was pleased he did the right thing because I was absolutely unprepared for what would happen if he served me the beer. When I emerged, the officers' expressions of dismay were obvious. I later discovered that one of them held a grudge against the bar's owner. It was my first introduction to the brutal side of policing.

After a few weeks of working undercover and making underage alcohol purchases, I became accustomed to the routine, and undercover jobs became second nature. It was a skill I would eventually apply as a Secret Service agent. The procedure was straightforward and efficient: walk in, get a beer, pay for it, pretend I forgot something, and leave. The officers would then rush in and issue the owner a criminal court summons. I fulfilled my duty effectively enough to be considered for reassignment to a new unit in the borough that would specialize on serial criminals, a line of work that I found extremely interesting given my academic background in psychology. The unit was known as the Pattern Identification Module, and its objective was to analyze data on big crimes to find patterns that might be conveyed to detective teams for further investigation. My job involved entering and analyzing data for hours at a time. In one case, I noticed a pattern of repeated home-invasion robberies in which the offender said the same thing every time he knocked on the door of a house he wanted to break into.

This early success in discovering trends in serial robbery cases provided me with a level of working independence that I had not previously experienced in my short tenure with the NYPD. This increased my credibility with the officers and sergeant I worked for, and they eventually permitted me to choose my own hours. With a new, flexible work schedule and the companionship of a decent team, I thoroughly enjoyed this assignment and spent the following two years working with them.

After a few months of working in the program, I befriended a fellow cadet named Marty. Marty enjoyed discussing politics on our journeys back to the police academy in Manhattan for continuous training, and he was the first to introduce me to conservatism's fundamental foundations. Although I was always interested in economics and politics, my grasp at the time was restricted, and my overall viewpoint was inadequate. Our lengthy, even heated discussions piqued my interest in why the important questions never appeared to be answered. Why were there areas of poverty despite decades of anti-poverty initiatives? Why does universal health care imply that some people received good care while others received mediocre care? Why did certain schools flourish while others failed terribly, despite guaranteed access? Marty had no idea at the time, but he piqued my attention, which would forever change my life.

As my college graduation date approached and my time as a police cadet came to an end, I began to plan for the next phase of my career with the NYPD. My contractual responsibility to serve as a police officer for two years after graduation from college was about to begin, and I was looking forward to the opportunity. The cadet program was a fascinating experience since it taught me about the organizational structures and psychology of police enforcement from the inside. The culture of law enforcement is distinct in that it distinguishes between individuals who carry firearms and those who do not, regardless of background or qualifications. Entering the police academy for the second time in the summer of 1997 was a smoother transition than my first entry into the cadet program as an adolescent. I found the training to be quite repetitious, so I spent the majority of my time developing relationships with my classmates.

After nearly nine months of academy training, we were prepared to select our "wish list" of precinct assignments before being assigned to an FTU, or "Field Training Unit." My FTU, where I would spend one month, was the 32nd Precinct in Harlem, a difficult assignment for a new officer. However, I chose the most challenging precinct inside the NYPD's borders for my first permanent assignment: the 75th Precinct in East New York, Brooklyn. I chose this famously dangerous precinct for two reasons: first, I knew the job would be difficult and enjoyed the challenge; second, I knew I'd get my wish because no one had requested the 75th.

Field training was the apex of the police academy experience, providing a welcome change from the monotony of the classroom and the rigid nature of the academy setting. The normal NYPD uniform was dark blue, but during field training, we were only allowed to wear our gray police academy suit. We were considered "rookies" by the police officers and residents of the precinct. Standing at my first roll call and hearing the chorus of "rookies, rookies" was a little humbling but amusing. It wasn't funny later on when almost everyone who passed by my foot post made similar remarks. I immediately learned that regardless of the outside weather, it was always a good idea to bring your standard-issue NYPD jacket, the same one worn by every other police officer, to cover up your gray shirt.

I was headed to my designated foot station when I noticed a man sitting on a store railing, smoking what seemed to be marijuana. I was both excited and worried because this was my first police action. As I approached him gently, he leaped down and started running. I screamed into my radio "10-85," which was the non-emergency request for help, and was immediately greeted by a cacophony of sirens as almost every police car in the precinct activated them simultaneously. I chased him down a city block until he was stopped by an officer in a car and handcuffed. Feeling relieved, I returned the man to the station with the accompanying policemen, who instead of praising me, lectured me on wasting police resources on "weed." The sharp lecture from the sergeant on duty at the precinct was even more emotionally distressing, but it taught me a lesson that would become a cornerstone of my political ideology. It taught me that holding an overly utopian perspective of the world has serious implications.

In an ideal society, recreational substances like marijuana would only exist for ethical purposes like medical treatment. However, the world is not ideal; legislative actions and lawmaking include trade-offs with serious implications. In a black-and-white world, engaging in a foot pursuit with a man smoking marijuana in public may appear to be the correct course of action. In the actual world, however, it entails police officers risking their lives by driving at high speeds, followed by the removal of additional police officials from the streets to assist with the administrative aspect of the arrest. Another tragic effect is the unfathomable harm caused by an arrest for what even the most ardent legal defenders would consider a minor violation. This man's life has been forever changed by the Internet and the indelible scar of a criminal record. The costs greatly outweigh the benefits.

Field training concluded with a brief goodbye to precinct personnel and an order to return to the police academy the following week for graduation. The New York Police Department's graduation ceremonies are spectacular. The ceremony is at Madison Square Garden, where hundreds of graduating recruits celebrate with their friends and families. It was the last time I saw many of my fellow academy recruits before we moved on to our careers with the department. Officer Stacie Williamson, a member of my training class, was shot and killed shortly after graduation, and Officer Daniel O'Sullivan was struck by a vehicle while assisting a stranded motorist and never recovered physically or psychologically, both tragic reminders of the daily dangers of wearing a badge and carrying a gun.

My permanent assignment to the 75th Precinct began with the same rookie hazing routines I had become accustomed to during both academy and field training. However, the hazing procedure in the 75th was far more severe than the one we encountered in the FTU. The 75th's policemen were street-hardened. This Brooklyn precinct had a statewide reputation for being the toughest place to work due to its regularly high crime rate and as a haven for troubled officers. The 75th included much of East New York, from the Belt Parkway to the entrance to Cypress Hills Street. This location was a world apart from Manhattan, the world's financial hub, and even the gentrified neighborhoods of Brooklyn couldn't have been more different. It was continually marred by drug conflicts, gang wars, racial intolerance, and urban ruin. It was heartbreaking to see, and as I began my duty with daily foot patrols in the most troubled areas of the precinct, I saw firsthand the true human cost of social policy, which most politicians and bureaucrats only read about in books. The devastation was nothing short of tragic: generational poverty and dependence, the likes of which are rarely seen in an affluent country like ours. The lives of the neighborhood residents were ignored by the media, politicians, and bureaucrats until something was required of them: votes, sound bites for the evening newscast while covering another crime scene, or a backdrop for another politician's rambling speech about a new piece of legislation he was supporting.

Chapter 3: IN THE LINE OF FIRE

Being a Police Officer in New York City is unlike any other job in the world. Things change quickly. The transition from acute dullness to adrenaline-inducing peril can occur in seconds. I was well aware that working the most dangerous shift in the precinct with the highest crime rate in New York City might soon change my ambitions to join a federal law enforcement agency or another area of work. This was never more clear than on a foot patrol on Fulton Street in the winter of 1998.

As the cop in pursuit began to outline his route, "northbound toward Fulton," I sensed they were quickly heading my way. The next thing I noticed was a set of headlights, followed by an extremely loud crash. The robber had driven the stolen car through a storefront's metal shutters, leaving the vehicle halfway inside. I ran to help my heart rate and was the first to enter the store. The thief exited the car and was attempting to flee when I tackled him and momentarily restrained him until the other officers arrived. These situations were all too typical in the 75th.

As my time in the 75th Precinct progressed, I became frustrated with the slow pace of the application procedure for federal law enforcement posts. Attending graduate school full-time at City University of New York and coping with nightly adrenaline rushes with the NYPD were wearing me down. By this point, I'd restricted my options to three federal agencies: the FBI (my preference), the DEA, and the US Secret Service.

After submitting the hefty paperwork, I happened to strike up a discussion with a woman while running on the treadmill at my local gym. She was an NYPD detective who worked with a task force squad that included a Secret Service agent. She went on to laud the Secret Service and the agent. She was entirely unaware that her brief meeting had changed my life. I began to actively pursue my advancement in the Secret Service application process, to the point where the administrative assistant assigned to the New York field office recruitment division recognized me by my first name. My continued involvement in the process undoubtedly irritated the recruitment section staff, but also accelerated the process. I took the written examination, went to the field office for an interview with a panel of agents, had a follow-up interview, underwent a complete medical examination, and endured the indignity of a full-scope polygraph examination all within six months.

Most Secret Service applicants dropped out after taking the polygraph test. Many did not pass, and I knew that because I did, my prospects of getting employed were excellent. It was the final step in the grueling process, and all I could do now was wait for a hiring decision. The waiting period was stressful since I sorely needed a change of scenery. It was challenging to balance graduate school and full-time job as a police officer. I routinely volunteered to labor in the precinct holding cells, an occupation that almost no one desired, because it provided me with small moments to read school material.

Working in the cells in a precinct with an extremely high crime rate was difficult. It was not uncommon to be berated by inmates during the eight-hour shift. I'd occasionally laugh at the inventiveness of some of those arrested. Standard insults were rarely effective, and because all convicts could hear each other, it became a race to see who could say the most bizarre things to the officer in the cells. I learnt to toughen up, which would come in handy later in politics. After weeks of captivity, I was desperate to get out and prayed nightly for that final phone call from the Secret Service. That phone call came in May 1999.

On June 21, 1999, I reported my first day as a Secret Service employee. I boarded the subway to the World Trade Center station and proudly ascended the escalator into the plaza, ready to face this new chapter of my life. I waited in the foyer of the Secret Service's flagship New York office with three other new hires—Lisa, Don, and Tom—

waiting to be summoned into the field office's inner sanctum, which was only open to Secret Service workers. When the door opened, Tim, our new supervisor, greeted us and began the lengthy indoctrination process into the Secret Service mentality.

Tim was a loud and often unpleasant man, but on protection assignments, these are qualities that might benefit an agent. His big frame and loud voice contributed to what some perceived as an imposing appearance. We spent the first month working under Tim's supervision, doing little more than filling out administrative paperwork, acting as the target of Tim's politically incorrect humor, and assisting the other agents in the office. We were not yet permitted to carry weapons or serve in any form of law enforcement role, so we waited for a new trainee class to begin at the Federal Law Enforcement Training Center (FLETC) in Brunswick, Georgia. When the formal news from Secret Service headquarters received that we would begin training at FLETC in July 1999, we were relieved that our next step had been verified. The comfort was short-lived, however, as bureau agents warned us that temperatures in Brunswick, Georgia, were in the upper 90s throughout most of July and August.

Tom and I agreed to go to FLETC, and I accompanied him for the entire fifteen-hour trip. Tom worked in financial services before joining the Secret Service, and we remained friends throughout our careers. Tom pursued a career in the Secret Service for the same broad reason I did: he wanted to do something bigger than what life had in store for him at the time. I found his sense of humor, often at my cost, to be a calming effect in the Secret Service's high-stress workplace. Being able to remain calm under tremendous stress is a vital ability in the Secret Service, and many of the agency's men and women, including Tom, used comedy to relieve tension on risky tasks.

Tom and I arrived at the facility about midnight and were assigned to our rooms, a rundown collection of dorms popularly known as the "Crack Houses." Needless to say, the dorms were outdated, and maintenance was badly insufficient. Despite the harsh name, I didn't mind the living arrangements. As a child, I lived in far worse conditions, so not having to pay rent was a relief.

The following day, we gathered with the rest of our Secret Service training class. These twenty-four men and women would be my companions and coworkers for the majority of the coming nine months. It was a formidable group, with personalities destined to conflict for all the right reasons. Everyone met the psychological criteria for type A classification. Our group consisted of Sue, the biochemist and outspoken perfectionist; Reggie, the strong, silent type who was always digesting his surroundings; Mike, the class clown but loyal friend to those loyal to him; and Chris, the former college football player who was the voice of reason when excitement overtook common sense.

The classroom element of the training was standard: law, investigative tactics, crime scene processing, and other courses geared to prepare us to be experts in finding criminals. Practical activities formed the foundation of the training and provided a welcome break from the monotony of regular lectures. The FLETC staff recruited actors to play certain parts in a pretend criminal investigation, which was integrated into all instructional activities. It was an excellent training technique, and the information we needed to acquire became very real to us as we learned about federal criminal investigations in the classroom and participated in an ongoing simulation. The entire process was evaluated, and I had one of the most competitive personalities around. I struggled to obtain the physical fitness award because of my class's outstanding aggregate fitness level, but I pushed for the academic prize until the final test. Sue and I had a pleasant rivalry for the entire nine weeks, and we would continuously question each other after each test, "What did you get?" Sue outscored me by less than a half-point on the course's final exam, which disappointed me. She and I would compete for the remainder of our lives, and while we never asked the question

"What did you get?" Again, we were constantly peering over our shoulders at each other in a race to the top.

The last several weeks of training were the simplest. The workload was easier, the Georgia heat subsided, and a nasty back injury I sustained during the first few days of training began to recover. I partially ruptured two spinal disks while performing a sit-up test, but instead of accepting a "recycle" (trainees who were injured were normally sent back to their originating field offices to rest and would begin anew in a new training class, referred to as "recycles"), I soldiered through the program. This was a costly mistake, since the injury never fully healed and haunted not only the rest of my Secret Service career, but also my ability to physically perform up to the high standards I had set for myself.

Although our homework was virtually finished in the last weeks, the internal struggle in the training class persisted. We all got along well, but living and working with the same group of people for nine weeks straight without a break is going to cause tension, both real and imagined. There was a love triangle; a cheating charge against one recruit who allegedly skipped a lap on the mile-and-a-half run test (cheating in the Secret Service is a never-forgivable offense); and periodic weekend fights in bars from Saint Simons Island to Savannah. These were genuine battles, but the imagined ones were far worse. Every day, someone seemed to come up with a new reason to be upset at a student labeled as a "slacker." The same few men and women swiftly established a reputation for lethargy and disinterest, and rumors about them spread like wildfire. As it turned out, some of those men and women would struggle throughout their careers, and one was fired shortly after graduation for an off-duty incident.

Graduation, despite being much anticipated, was a letdown. The brief ceremony took place in the chapel on the FLETC grounds, but we still had an eleven-week training course to finish at the Secret Service training site in Laurel, Maryland. Most of us were pleased to shake hands and say, "See you in Maryland." The eleven-week term marked the second and last phase of our instruction, and the class was excited to get started.

I was captivated by every classroom course we attended, and I was as struck by the agency's emphasis on marksmanship and gun proficiency. Handling a firearm anywhere near the President of the United States is a serious duty, and the Secret Service places a high value on firearm proficiency. We were scheduled for range time almost every day of the training. The instruction was tough and unlike anything I had ever seen at the New York Police Academy or FLETC.

Both the classroom and firearms instructors were knowledgeable, and each had intriguing experiences to relate about touring the world with presidents ranging from Nixon to Clinton. During breaks in training, we'd gather around and listen to their bizarre stories. The instructors were all unabashedly proud of their work and the organization that had become such a vital part of their life, and this filtered down to the pupils. Because of its unique twin role of protection and complex investigations, the Secret Service has developed a distinct culture. Embedding this culture in every student trainee is a vital goal for any teacher, as I was reminded several times when I returned as an instructor years later.

Dan E. was an instructor who every agent in my training class remembers. Dan eventually wrote an essay about his experience in the Secret Service and was as tough a person as I had ever met. A former US Marine, he would not hesitate to kick sand in your face on the difficult 200-yard obstacle course if he believed you weren't giving it your all. He valued diligent workers but had no patience for whiners or excuse makers. This made him a popular target for management's ire, since they did not appreciate his candor. Ironically, when I began to speak publicly about the Secret Service over a decade later during my candidacy for the United States Senate, most media outlets that requested an interview would contact either me or Dan, depending on who was available.

Explaining the course was usually tedious when I called home and told friends about my daily routine, but knowing about the intricacies hidden in something as simple as a $1 bill was eye-opening. We strolled through the money-making process, spending time at a secret facility where the proprietary paper used to print our currency is manufactured, and then followed the paper to the Bureau of Engraving and Printing in Washington, DC, to see it transformed into US cash. During this phase of the training, I felt the pleasure of my first flight in an airplane. Growing up in a financially challenged home, flight travel was never a possibility for me.

Credit card fraud classes were more extensive and sophisticated than the rest of the material. Stealing someone's credit card information was originally a straightforward task that has since turned into a technologically sophisticated criminal operation. When credit cards were first introduced into the US market, firms would manually process them with paper carbon copies of the card. When these duplicates were discarded, criminals recognized an opportunity, and the art of "Dumpster diving" emerged. Criminals would steal carbon copy slips with credit card details from businesses' dumpsters and then create phony credit cards using the stolen numbers. With the advent of totally electronic processing, more sophisticated theft methods evolved. We learnt about "skimming," which occurs when a criminal grabs your credit card during a transaction and swipes it through the business processor before storing the information from the magnetic strip on his own device. The information from the magnetic strip is then electronically encoded on a new card.

In addition to the financial crime classes, we were gradually introduced to the tactics used by the Secret Service to safeguard the president, its most well-known task. The AOP (assault on principal) training, in which an actor impersonating the president was exposed to several attack scenarios, was rigorous and traumatic. Each day brought a new scenario in which our unlucky role actor was shot at, stabbed, punched, tormented, and generally manhandled throughout the simulations. The Secret Service favors realism in its training environment, employing weapons that fire "Simunition" bullets. Simunition cartridges use plastic bullets that are tougher than standard paintballs and contain a waxy, pigmented component that alerts others that you have been shot. You, on the other hand, know instantly when you've been shot with a Simunition round because the agony is excruciating, and getting hit in sensitive parts like your hands is an experience you'll never forget, especially in cold weather when the wax hardens. Training with these rounds teaches rookie agents how to rapidly go behind cover and avoid being "cowboys."

During one practice in the Secret Service tactical village, our protectee came under heavy fire from some of the instructors. I recall being hit repeatedly and scrambling for cover as quickly as possible. I was able to fit my six-foot, 200-pound bulk behind a fire hydrant on the street and fire back, striking one of the teachers at least three times. He backed off, we kept the "president" alive for the exercise, and I ended up with a collection of twenty-plus deep purple welts as a memento of what I had learned that day.

Our training class was set to graduate in December 1999, and tensions in the law enforcement community around the country were high. The fear of a global computer network failure during the Y2K scare gripped the country, and the threat of terrorism grew enormously. My classmates were eager to graduate and begin working. Everyone was thinking about their final exams and physical fitness tests.

The Secret Service's physical fitness training is rigorous, and graduation requires passing five tests: maximum sit-ups and push-ups in one minute, maximum chin-ups (no time limit), a flexibility test, and a one-and-a-half-mile run. I was keen to obtain an "excellent" on all of the test components, and I was well over the criteria for my age in all but the run, where I finished just seconds faster than the needed time for an "excellent" (ten minutes and sixteen seconds). In between studying for final exams in protection, protection intelligence, and financial crimes, I ran whenever possible. I enjoyed running with Sean, a classmate and former military police officer who was amusingly robotic in his approach to any work. He approached every difficulty or assignment objectively, and he had won the respect of the class for his ability to remain calm and adapt to any challenge put at us. I ran with him frequently because, regardless of the weather or our exhaustion, he never grumbled, which helped me stay focused.

I was nervous the day of my final fitness test. I believed I couldn't leave the academy without excelling in every area, and the run was weighing hard on me. The run was the final part of the exam that day, and it was cold and pouring, making it difficult to breathe. I pushed myself hard in the remaining components, nearly doubling the requirements for an exceptional score, but I was exhausted. My breathing became heavy within the first quarter mile of the run, but I continued to run at a pace way outside my comfort zone. And I paid the price: the second and third quarter miles were like jogging across wet concrete. My legs felt like anchors, but I was not going to graduate without feeling satisfied that I had accomplished this goal. The last quarter mile was the most agonizing experience I've ever had, and I knew if I slowed down even a step, I'd fall short of the time limit. I grabbed my last bit of energy and sprinted the final fifty yards to the finish line. The instructor roared, "Ten-sixteen." The session ended on a positive note.

Chapter 4: THE END OF THE CLINTON ERA

I started my Secret Service career at the New York field office, but after graduating from the training program, I was sent to the Melville, New York, field office. The news was disappointing; I had expected to return to the city where I grew up and work in the field office. Tom also received some surprising news: he was reassigned to our office at John F. Kennedy International Airport in Queens.

Tom and I both recognized that the New York City office, as the Secret Service's flagship office, handled the majority of high-profile criminal investigations and protection assignments. The Melville field office, located in Suffolk County, about thirty miles from town, has a reputation for being "slow." Some of my New York agency pals referred to it as the "Melville Country Club." This reputation abruptly shifted in September 1999, when then-President Bill Clinton and his wife, Hillary, bought a home in the tranquil Westchester town of Chappaqua, New York. Rumors quickly spread that the first lady will run for the United States Senate seat of retiring Senator Daniel Patrick Moynihan, a New York legend.

Marty, the agent in charge of the Melville field office, was a "by the book" manager. He was a genuinely pious and principled guy who stood firm in his support for his men and the Secret Service mission. Marty knew a firestorm was on its way when he learned the Clintons had purchased the Chappaqua mansion. A bid for the US Senate by the wife of the current president of the United States would have been a massive protective assignment for the agents and management of the New York field office, but they had the people to handle it. The Melville field office had just nine agents. We simply did not have enough staffing to handle Mrs. Clinton's numerous campaign visits, and the majority of the agents in the office had less than two years of Secret Service protection experience. A visit by the first lady was a highly organized and elaborate operation that was normally handled by veteran agents with experience in the Presidential Protective Division (PPD).

The PPD was a psychologically taxing environment, with agents normally having at least seven years of experience and being hand-picked as the finest of the best. They had no patience for new agents with no expertise in "the big show" (a euphemism some PPD agents used for presidential protection). There was no historical precedent for this, adding to the complexity of an already challenging operational necessity. No current first lady had previously run for office, thus any protection model would have to be designed with intricate political considerations in mind.

Security is more than just putting a protectee in a bulletproof glass box. Security plans must be created to provide a level of protection while enabling access to the principal. When that principle runs for political office, it adds layers of access that other protectees do not have, because the fear of losing an election causes both candidates and their staff to behave strangely.

I could see from our first meeting with Scott, a polished and well-respected PPD agent assigned to the first lady, that this assignment would necessitate a "on-the-job" training component that was nothing like the conventional program the Secret Service established for incoming agents. I'd have to quickly learn how to apply what I'd learned in class to real-world, high-stakes scenarios, and the repercussions of failing were unimaginable. In the Secret Service, reputation management is an important skill to learn rapidly. Complaining about working circumstances is frowned upon, and the peer pressure on individuals who choose to break this rule is severe. Dealing with the PPD so early in my career could have been a fantastic opportunity, or it could have meant the end of my career. If I had excelled, it would have been in the eyes of fellow agents, who, because of their seniority and prestigious position on the PPD, would most likely have become my superiors in the near future. However, had I failed, the consequences would have been irreversible. There were further considerations when working with the several municipal police departments in Long Island's Nassau and Suffolk counties. Their participation was crucial to our achievement. They all had different notions about how to properly guard perimeters and conduct motorcades, and I rapidly learned how to perform domestic diplomacy with our law enforcement colleagues.

I was both thrilled and humbled to be involved in the Clinton campaign and on the front lines of what would become the most costly Senate battle in US history. Not a week went by without PPD operations in Washington informing us that the first lady would be visiting, and we had no days off. She was not polling well on Long Island, and while she did not need to win either of the two counties, she did need to perform well. The political drama surrounding the campaign was fierce, and it swiftly evolved into a national referendum on the Clintons.

Clinton's original opponent, former New York City Mayor Rudy Giuliani, dropped out of the race early in the summer of 2000, but her campaign continued to confront problems. Charges of "carpetbagger" (an oddly weak charge that would be thrown at me in my 2012 race for the United States Senate) were relentless, but watching the Clinton machine in operation from behind the scenes was like taking a PhD-level campaign management course. Even seemingly minor situations made front-page news. The campaign's choice of a vehicle, which is usually a non-issue among both the Secret Service and the press, became a story when they chose a two-tone brown Ford conversion van, which differed greatly from the president and his family's fleet of black limousines. The vehicle's brown color earned it the nickname "Scooby-Doo" among the Secret Service. Looking back, I see the decision to choose the dull brown van as a stroke of political genius. Every news outlet shot of Mrs. Clinton's arrivals showed her exiting this pretty middle-class-looking van. This resonated with me years later, when I ran for office, and I would continuously remind my team that campaigns are about "sound bites and snapshots." Short statements and photos can tell a story to a large group of voters in ways that protracted speeches cannot.

The Clintons had a narrow inner circle and preferred to have everything done their way, with few exceptions. This being my first political campaign from the "inside," I was originally startled by the level of sycophantic conduct displayed by elected politicians eager to be identified with a winner. When the Clinton campaign announced her plans to visit Long Island, Marty started receiving phone calls. Every locally elected person on the Democratic side of the political fence would demand for access, which Marty had no intention of allowing, and when Mrs. Clinton arrived, they would all queue up like schoolchildren eager to appear in a photograph that would be published in the newspaper. Seeing this on a weekly basis puts a stain on my heart about the genuine motivations of those seeking public office, which has yet to be washed away.

When Long Island congressional representative Rick Lazio was named the presumptive Republican nominee, succeeding Rudy Giuliani, the Clinton campaign faced increased pressure to recover votes on Long Island. In addition to the growing frequency of visits to the area overseen by our small Secret Service office, the stress of dealing with the local police became an issue.

Security is an art form, not a science, and the campaign did not want to burden all local police assets with each visit. The Clinton campaign did not want to deplete local police resources, and the constant issue of the candidate seeming "accessible" caused a number of uncomfortable times in my interactions with police. Although protection service was arduous, the local police officers enjoyed being a part of the ongoing buzz around a high-profile protectee, and the overtime pay further fueled their desire to be present when the first lady visited town. It was difficult to request that the police stand down when the security was adequate and no more assets were required. They sincerely wanted to help, and as a former uniformed cop myself, I understood their situation.

As November's election approached, the campaign became increasingly challenging. The pressure to win was immense. A loss would damage Clinton's name and end a potential second legacy before it ever began. The stress was particularly noticeable among the crew. I found the personnel to be full political opposites to my conservative leanings, but they were passionate, loyal followers of their cause, which I secretly appreciated.

Despite my appreciation for their efforts, we had regular disagreements in the last months of the campaign. Their duty is to get their candidate elected, and while security is a priority for them, our techniques are sometimes misconstrued. Secret Service agents are in charge of reviewing intelligence reports, communicating with local police, and putting together a security plan that considers the protector's needs. The staff seemed to believe that some of our tactics were superfluous, and the battles became boring. Marty gave me a strong warning for one particular tactic. I felt it was a great solution to a security problem we were experiencing at a nearby institution.

I was tasked with securing an indoor speech site for Mrs. Clinton on a university campus, and I noted right away that there was an adjacent building with windows that provided a direct view of the stage. As a Secret Service agent, you soon learn to see anything as a possible problem. If a gunman were stationed in one of those rooms, he would be well inside rifle range, which worried me tremendously. I didn't have enough security officers between campus police and Secret Service agents to station someone in that building, so I had to come up with a unique alternative.

After a few hours of strolling through the site with the topic on my mind, I had a lightbulb moment. I considered using synthetic snow.

I remembered my mother spray-painting faux snow on the windows of our apartment above the bar. I asked the university host if he wouldn't mind buying some artificial snow and sprinkling it on the windows to obscure the view of the building. She agreed and didn't seem upset by my request. On the day of the visit, I patiently waited in front of the scheduled arrival spot for the motorcade to come, which is always the most stressful portion of any visit. I muttered a quick prayer, hoping for the best, as I always did, as the motorcade approached and came to a stop just where we had planned. I led the swarm of agents, staffers, host committee members, and local politicians into the chamber, only to discover that the windows had a dark covering that bore no resemblance to the fake snow we had described. Putting this knowledge aside, I concentrated on the remainder of the visit, listening to Mrs. Clinton's remarks, guiding her through an uneventful rope line full of eager youngsters, and returning her to the car.

Proud of my work for the visit, I thanked everyone before gathering my equipment and leaving. It wasn't until the next day that I learned I'd created a stir on campus. Instead of faking snow, the institution purchased black spray paint and sprayed the windows with it. The university maintenance personnel had made numerous attempts to remove it but were having difficulty. The university staff then called Marty to praise him for his assistance and brought up the paint. Marty was upset and informed me immediately. That day, I learnt that when the Secret Service demands something, it will be done. Nevertheless, it is my obligation to guarantee that it is done without excessive burden. I apologized to the university and took the lesson with me.

On election night in 2000, my campaign experience with the Clintons ended. It was bittersweet. I not only learned vital things about our techniques from the PPD agents assigned to the first lady, but I also discovered a lot about myself. I pushed myself harder than I ever had in my life and came out uninjured. After all of the visits, motorcades, travels, and threats, Mrs. Clinton was still alive and well, with no close calls during the campaign.

But there was no rest for our tired bodies on election night. The Melville field office was assigned to work at the Hyatt in New York City, where Mrs. Clinton, her staff, and a mob of supporters would congregate to monitor the results. Personally, I hoped for a national Republican triumph that night, and for the party to win the New York Senate seat. Although I would have given my life gladly for Mrs. Clinton as a Secret Service agent, I was still a Republican who realized the party needed to win both nationally and in New York. That night, I received minute-by-minute briefings on all of the current races from the Clinton crew, who were feigning apathy the entire time to avoid causing a spectacle if Mrs. Clinton lost. Adding to the craziness of the night, our handheld metal detector failed at the checkpoint I was guarding, forcing me to manually pat down incoming guests. My first victim was actor Ben Affleck, who was kind-hearted about it.

As the night progressed and exit poll results poured in, it was clear that the first lady would be declared the winner. When the race was called for Mrs. Clinton The entire hotel appeared to shake with elation. I was politically disappointed, but I was moved by the genuine emotion from the campaign team I had grown to know well. They clearly believed in their cause as much as I did. However, the presidential election was a completely different situation.

I was relieved by another agent late that night and returned to my room, still unsure if the next president would be Texas Governor George W. Bush or Vice President Al Gore. This action had serious consequences for me, politically and emotionally. The Clinton team was firmly telling me that Gore "had it," but some of the doubters were quietly noting that it was "not over." I was devastated when several media outlets declared Florida for Al Gore. I felt like the Republican Party's obituary had just been written.

The next day, I awoke believing that the first lady had won her Senate election in New York and that Al Gore had been elected as our new president. When I switched on the television cable news channel, I was surprised to see Florida back in the "undecided" column. What followed was over a month of speculation and well-documented political drama, with serious implications for the Secret Service. With no room for error in its planning, the Secret Service was forced to build a presidential security footprint for two president-elects, George W. Bush and Al Gore.

Planning for a single presidential transition is challenging enough for both the White House and the Secret Service, but planning for two was never contemplated. The pandemonium ended in mid-December 2000, when the Supreme Court halted the recount of presidential ballots, declaring George W. Bush the winner.

Chapter 5: 9/11

SEPTEMBER 11, 2001, was a peaceful morning in our Long Island workplace. Tony, Joe, and I were organizing a search warrant and arrest for an Internet scammer who was "selling" jewels on eBay (but not the actual gems). While we were discussing the arrest mechanics of the operation, Tom, a senior agent within the office who had earned a reputation for calm and who loved to remark, "Take it easy" whenever he saw an agent becoming emotional, raced into my office saying, "Someone just bombed the World Trade Center." He was on the phone with our New York office at 7 World Trade Center when the first plane hit the North Tower, and the dispatcher he was dealing with thought it was a bomb.

After learning that the World Trade Center had been attacked again (Muslim terrorists having detonated a truck bomb in its basement garage in 1993), we dropped our arrest papers and rushed into the back of the office, where Marty had a cable news station on... and nothing. There was no report of a bomb in the World Trade Center. Marty started changing channels, and I remember him looking up at The View and saying, "I don't see anything."

At that point, we saw the dreaded "Breaking News" slide across the screen, and a live newscaster interrupted the show, seemingly unprepared for what he was going to deliver. I don't recall any of his or anybody else's statements in the room at the time because I was so focused on the television. The live sight of a gaping hole in the side of the World Trade Center's North Tower appeared strange. I had just been with some Secret Service friends to the Windows on the World restaurant on the top floors of the North Tower the week before, admiring the incredible 360-degree views. I also started my career with Tom, Lisa, and Don in the lobby of our 7 World Trade Center New York field office, and I would often go back to the day I ascended the escalator into the World Trade Center plaza after being hired. It was one of my finest moments, and the plaza still evokes thoughts of regeneration and kindness. So it was weird to see papers and building bits fall onto the plaza below. Marty, who rarely exhibited emotion and had admonished me numerous times throughout my time working for him for wearing my feelings on my sleeve, was plainly as shaken by the incident as the rest of us. His normally stern expression telegraphed the rage we all felt but didn't utter.

Any mention of the impending arrest was immediately forgotten. One of the longest, most emotionally agonizing days of my life had just begun. After swiftly debating with Marty the best method for us to assist, we decided to travel to our satellite field office at JFK Airport in Queens, where Tom was assigned, and begin the process of locating the hundreds of Secret Service people who worked at the World Trade Center. As we walked out, employees from the other firms in the office complex were crying and desperately attempting to contact loved ones. Cell phone networks were congested, and making an outgoing call was practically impossible. As I urgently attempted to contact my brother Joseph, the inability to make a call had an emotional toll on me.

Joseph was an emergency medical technician for the New York City Fire Department. Knowing my brother, I was confident he had hurried to lower Manhattan to help. My cell phone rang as I opened the car door, and I looked down, hoping it was Joseph, but it was really my father. I'd never known him to be an openly emotional man, but he was crying on the phone, clearly thinking about my brother. It would be hours before I heard from Joseph, but we needed to hurry to the JFK office to help.

Manny, a senior agent in the office, greeted us at JFK and informed us that there were hundreds of unaccounted for agents, and that we should begin paging them on their work-issued pagers and crossing them off the list when they arrived at work. As they arrived one by one, they all shared stories of unimaginable fear. They all described the horror of seeing panicked people in the buildings choose to leap rather than be burned alive, and the noises of bodies crashing against the pavement. I'll never forget these stories, and for years following, whenever I checked into a high-rise hotel, I'd look out the window and envision the anguish the victims of this attack felt when they decided to leap.

There were other stories of heroism told about the heroic men and women of the Secret Service's New York field office who, rather than fleeing, stayed at the plaza to provide medical aid. Two agents, John and Tom, who ran into the North Tower despite several warnings to evacuate people who couldn't get out on their own, stick out to me as powerful examples of the bravery displayed by many that sad day. Both men were inside the North Tower when the South Tower collapsed. They were blinded by dust and debris as they attempted to descend the North Tower's dimly lit stairs, having heard the sound of the fall. These two guys saved people's lives, yet they rarely, if ever, talk about it. Their heroism was quiet.

By late afternoon on Tuesday, September 11, only a few names remained on my list of New York field office personnel who could be accounted for. With each passing minute, our worry mounted that their phone call would never arrive. We didn't overtly discuss their potential destruction; instead, we speculated on why they weren't responding to the pages we sent out. Finally, we received a call from an agent indicating the location of a large group of missing agents. We crossed a list of names. Some of the agents had evacuated individuals by boat and arrived in New Jersey, but their pagers had fallen off, becoming casualties of the turmoil.

Despite the relief of finding the agents, we still had two names left on the list. Kevin, a buddy of mine, and I briefly worked together in the Melville office. Kevin and Marty weren't best friends during Kevin's stay in Melville, but they learnt to get along. Kevin was a seasoned veteran who rarely held back his thoughts—quite the contrary of Marty, who was difficult to read. I had grown to appreciate Kevin, and the notion of what might have happened to him was difficult to accept. I was relieved when we received a phone call informing us that he had been on assignment in Lagos, Nigeria and was well. There was one name on the list that was never checked. As the evening approached, it became clear that Craig Miller would be the lone member of the Secret Service to never return home following the terrorist assaults. Master Special Officer Craig Miller died that dreadful day. Given his history of service to the country in both the US Army and the Secret Service, it is believed that he died in the World Trade Center plaza while providing medical aid to victims when the South Tower collapsed. Craig Miller died a hero while serving his country in a time of need.

Although the planes only hit the North and South Towers, the subsequent collapse caused significant damage to the adjacent structures. The New York field office was on the ninth story of 7 World Trade Center. As the fires raged within the structure, it became structurally unsafe and collapsed at 5:00 p.m. that day, taking everything with it. All of the criminal case files, firearms, equipment, radios, armored vehicles, and agents' personal belongings were missing. As I went home from the JFK office that night, I made one more visit at the Melville office and noticed Marty conversing with an agent I recognized from New York. The agent was covered in the now-famous white dust from the towers' collapse and carrying a bag containing a Heckler & Koch MP5 submachine gun. When I questioned him why he had the MP5, he said, "It may be the only thing that made it out of the building."

In the days and weeks following the assaults, the special agents of the New York office's dissatisfaction with Secret Service management's response exacerbated the anguish and horror. As time passed and our detached leaders, who rarely left their sheltered offices in our DC headquarters, did not visit the site of the attack, the indignation escalated into an open rage rarely witnessed in an organization proud of its culture of discipline and secrecy. It was my first experience with the contrast between the emotional response of working-class Secret Service officers and the cynical attitude of the "cocktail party" management class. Bureaucracy breeds a lack of accountability, which breeds an apathy that I subsequently discovered is widespread throughout the United States government.

Representative Steny Hoyer was among the Washington leaders visiting New York. The congressman had a reputation for supporting the Secret Service, and he personally visited our New York office workers, who are now dispersed around Manhattan in various facilities, to express his support. This was my first encounter with Representative Hoyer, whom I would later meet in my political career when I supported his opponent in the 2012 general election for Maryland's Fifth Congressional District. Although I disagreed with Representative Hoyer politically, I will never forget his outstanding commitment to our cause following those sad events.

On a very personal note, I met my future wife, Paula, just days before 9/11. She worked for the Securities Industry Association (SIA), which has offices next to the World Trade Center buildings. When she did not return my calls on September 11, I was concerned she might have been a victim. However, by chance, she had decided at the last minute to see her mother in Nevada, and she was moved by my repeated messages checking on her. Her building was unharmed, but she would be able to see the hallowed grounds of Ground Zero from her office starting that day.

It wasn't long before New York City's nerves were tried again, and Paula's safety inspired me to act. Only two months after the tragic September 11 terrorist attacks, a jet crashed shortly after takeoff into the Rockaway district in Queens, New York.

I was in a neighborhood gym on Woodhaven road in Forest Hills, Queens, when the incident occurred. I immediately felt my Secret

Service pager vibrate and heard the boom of dozens of emergency vehicles rushing down the road. Terrorism was quickly suspected, and with no immediate reason to believe differently, I ran to my car and drove to Paula's workplace on the edge of Ground Zero, fearing it would be targeted again. I begged her to escort me out of her office. She reluctantly agreed, and despite her supervisor's belief that I was exaggerating, we ran to my car, where I drove her home. It was eventually discovered that a catastrophic mix of weather and pilot error caused the jet to crash into the Rockaway neighborhood, killing all 260 passengers and five bystanders on the ground.

Chapter 6: AN ASSASSIN AMONG US

A HIGH-LEVEL MEETING of the United Nations General Assembly was always a logistical nightmare for the Secret Service. Planning and implementing a full-spectrum security plan for over a hundred heads of state and their wives, as well as the president of the United States, in New York City's packed streets leaves a security team with little options and makes them an ideal target for an assassin or terrorist. These problems were much more pronounced after September 11. The 2002 United Nations General Assembly would be a test of the Secret Service's improved operational procedures and contingency planning efforts since the tragic 9/11 terrorist attacks.

By 2002, I had quickly advanced through the ranks and was one of the senior agents in the protected intelligence squad. My new job after the Melville field office was the New York field office, which is presently located in downtown Brooklyn following the loss of our office space at 7 World Trade Center. When we moved in, the new field office was still under construction, and the agents in the office were still dealing with the aftermath of the terrorist attacks, making the dismal "under construction" atmosphere more emotionally demanding than any other remodeling project. The purple walls and abandoned equipment from the previous tenant, who had departed in a hurry, gave it a distinctively unserious, noninstitutional appearance, exacerbating the already low workplace mood.

When the assignments for the UN General Assembly began to arrive and Scott, the backup (the second in command of each squad within a field office), posted them, we rushed to find out who would be covering each dignitary. The Secret Service was a collection of alpha guys and girls, and everyone on the squad hoped to be assigned to a high-risk country. There was no greater task for a field office agent than properly completing advance work for a foreign head of state designated as a high-risk protectee.

I was excited to see where I would be assigned and was overjoyed when I saw the name of a country on the board with my name next to it, which had a high threat level. This particular head of state rose to power in a coup, and his country's sole constant was volatility. My mission was to conduct extensive study on the threats to this country, its leader, and the UN in general, and then present a threat assessment based on all of this material so that the members of the advance team could devise appropriate countermeasures. Dave, the lead advance agent, was known for his meticulous work and willingness to put in long hours, so I was confident that he would use the information I supplied to develop a successful security strategy.

I spent about a week organizing the visit and had extensive but acrimonious discussions with the foreign country's staff. The crew, like many others, wanted more automobiles in the procession than we could safely secure. Motorcade length is a symbol of power in the business and, in some cases, adolescent politics of dignitary protection, and the difficult discussions to shorten the motorcade lasted days. Despite the lengthy disputes over minute matters, the protector's entrance in the country was pleasantly uneventful.

After we were informed that the protectee was "in for the night" and would have no further movements from the hotel, I went to my hotel room to try to get some well-deserved sleep, but that was not to be. My Blackberry rang around two o'clock in the morning, and the agent in charge of our detail, Roy, informed me that sources were relaying newly acquired information to Secret Service headquarters about a plot to assassinate our protectee, which was set to take place within the next few days. Roy told me that the objective was to disguise an assassin as a member of the press traveling with the head of state and his staff, then kill him with a pistol.

Being awakened late at night with such knowledge is every agent's greatest nightmare. The advance team bears the responsibility for the life of the assigned protectee collectively, yet each member feels the pressure to perform individually. Secret Service administration does not micromanage their agents and allows them considerable responsibility, but that responsibility comes with a cost. Agents are responsible for any failure to perform the mission at hand, and failure must be avoided at all costs. I spent the next hour on the phone with Roy, discussing the heightened security measures we would put in place to prevent any potential assassination plot. We had already established and implemented a thorough press screening process to verify they were "clean" (i.e., free of weapons or explosives), but out of prudence, we made some strategic changes. I recommended to Roy that we sweep the press at each halt. The standard approach was to sweep them once and then appoint an agent to keep an eye on them to ensure they remained clean. Given the gravity of this danger and the severe geopolitical and personal ramifications if it is successful, I believe this is a necessary nuisance for the press and staff, who would undoubtedly be unhappy with the additional time these measures would add to their daily schedules.

The next day began with heightened anxiety among the detail members. We ensured that the early scan of the press entourage was thorough, and we were relieved to find no weapons. When we got to the first stop and instructed the press entourage to go through another scan, I could see their amazement at this unexpected request. Members of the press are inherently curious people, and they began to wonder what was wrong. When prompted to repeat the security sweep process at each subsequent stop, the questions became more numerous.

One of the most difficult aspects of the Secret Service protection program is the inability to demonstrate that we stopped an assassination. Assassins do not extend the courtesy of informing you when you have destroyed their plans. Throughout the day, we noticed the press pool diminishing with each stop. We'll never know for certain whether this was the consequence of growing annoyance with the smothering security or a prospective assassin being defeated by our security scheme, but in either case, our objective was completed. We took the protectee back to his plane at John F. Kennedy International Airport and watched as he safely exited the country, keeping in mind that there are no rewards for projected success, only penalties for failure.

Chapter 7: TRAINING THE NEXT GENERATION

I seemed ALWAYS LOOKING FOR ACTIVITIES TO MAINTAIN A HIGH LEVEL OF PHYSICAL FITNESS, and the developing mixed martial arts movement seemed the ideal fit. It blended the strength and endurance of collegiate wrestling with the skill demands of boxing and the strategic gamesmanship of Brazilian jiu-jitsu. Conveniently, in 2002, the Secret Service training center in Maryland advertised a post for a control tactics instructor. The majority of Secret Service hand-to-hand combat training was based on boxing instruction, although this approach had a number of tactical issues. The most basic concern was that all agents were armed with a handgun and an extendable baton to avoid a stand-up hand-to-hand confrontation. Furthermore, during training, we frequently discovered that when a pupil lacked boxing abilities, he or she learned only one thing: how to take a good thrashing. Introducing mixed martial arts alleviated many of these issues. It was successful on the ground and remarkably low-impact.

Although I only had three years of experience as a special agent when the control tactics instructor position was advertised, I believed that this would be an excellent opportunity to advance my career in a new direction. I applied for the open position and impatiently awaited a response. Marty, my former supervisor at the Melville field office, was kind and made several phone calls to headquarters on my behalf. These calls are an unfortunate but necessary aspect of the Secret Service culture. Merit accounts for around 70% of the selection process for any position inside the Secret Service, while the other 30% involves having the right person make the right phone call at the right moment. This is not a work trait specific to the Secret Service. Throughout government employment, there is a strong emphasis on making the right contacts to improve your career. Thick federal bureaucracies are notorious for this kind of organizational progress.

Here is how it works: Government employee A promotes his friend, the less senior government employee B, into a position with the understanding that when government employee A retires and moves into a lobbying or private sector position where he can leverage his inside connections, he can rely on government employee B to provide him with access to government contacts and largesse.

The personal aspect of my probable transfer was going to be more difficult. Paula and I were still dating at the time, and despite some early obstacles, our love was strengthening. Paula loved living in New York and was concerned about the consequences for our relationship if I left without her. She often said to me, "amor de lejos es amor de pendejos," which is an old, slightly off-color Spanish term that means "love from afar is love for fools." This beautifully summarized her attitude on long-distance relationships.

I chose to wait until I was notified of a choice before telling her about the employment. In late fall 2002, Marty called to congratulate me on my transfer to the James J. Rowley Secret Service Training Center in Prince George's County, Maryland. I was overjoyed, but also concerned about Paula's reaction, for I would not go without her. I called her right away and, after some hesitation, told her, "I've been sent to DC."

Based on the delay in her reaction, I concluded she was upset. I was shocked and delighted to hear joy in her voice, and the fact that she was willing to make a dramatic move. Even though we had just been dating for a year, she said she would check with her SIA supervisor to see if a move to their Washington, DC office was possible. She also agreed to go with me on my house-hunting vacation to Maryland. I knew if she left me, the heartbreak would be permanent, so I was relieved when she agreed to "take a look" at Maryland.

After conducting a thorough cost-benefit analysis of residing in Maryland versus Virginia or Washington, I chose Maryland. The situation seemed wonderful to me. Robert Ehrlich had just been elected as the state's first Republican governor in over thirty years, and, while the legislature was largely dominated by Democrats, the state itself offered a little bit of everything: good schools, a major city in Baltimore, proximity to my workplace, Catoctin Mountain Park, Deep Creek Lake, the Chesapeake Bay, Annapolis, and much more that I would discover while living there.

Paula and I left on our house-hunting journey in November 2002, enthused about the prospects. Owning a home was something I had never contemplated as a child, and now I was on a trip to purchase one. It was a new adventure for us. After a week of looking at houses in various communities, we decided on a home in Severna Park. With its white facade, blue shutters, and expansive front yard, it was the slice of middle-class heaven Paula and I had been looking for our entire lives.

I first went to Maryland by myself, while Paula remained in New York for an additional month to complete her work for SIA's New York office. I arrived at work eager to start in the control tactics unit, but was disappointed to be temporarily allocated to the investigative tactics section. The section was low on personnel, so I was assigned to fill in as an instructor until a permanent replacement could be found.

I had recently concluded a nearly two-year investigation into a huge credit card fraud ring linked to international terrorism, so I was well-versed in the subtleties of major federal investigations. After a week of teaching classes with no prior lecturing experience, the section's supervisor, Bob, was impressed with my understanding of the subject and shifted me to the section full time. I enthusiastically accepted the new assignment. I appreciated working with Bob, who had been with the Secret Service for about 20 years, both in our investigative sections and in the Vice Presidential Protective Division (VPD). Bob was constantly smiling, unlike Marty, who seemed to be internally pondering over something. Bob had come from the VPD, and in Secret

Service culture, you are either a Presidential Protective Division (PPD) agent or a VPD agent, and this identity is permanent. It didn't matter if you started at VPD as a rank-and-file agent and subsequently was promoted to PPD as a supervisor; you'd always be known as a "VP guy."

The training center's investigative tactics training curriculum required a comprehensive redesign. With the addition of another new agent to the section, a tough-as-nails Marine veteran named Tim, we were ready to abandon the old program and begin again. Tim and I had quite different backgrounds, but we quickly became friends. He was a country lad, and I was a New Yorker, so he called me "Big City." I chuckled at the moniker and eventually came to accept it. As someone who grew up primarily in New York City, I found Tim's stories about shooting squirrels in his backyard with a.22 rifle as a child amusing. This type of conduct would have resulted in your arrest in New York City and was unprecedented. Ironically, while growing up in diametrically opposed surroundings, we both had broadly similar worldviews and instructional approaches. We valued leadership and personal responsibility in pupils and would recognize those who, while not the most proficient, exhibited the best character.

Tim and I determined that if we were going to revamp this training program, we wanted to make it cutting-edge. We sought the best personnel for each specialized subject area and participated in training programs to understand the most recent investigative techniques in the field. Tim attended an interview and interrogation school in Florida, whereas I attended a surveillance school conducted by a major intelligence agency. We both requested assistance from the Drug Enforcement Administration in updating the program's covert methods portion. The makeover was a year-long process, and we were both quite proud of the finished result, which combined the best knowledge from brilliant subject matter experts to create a high-quality training program.

Our responsibilities did not stop with curriculum redesign. Following an introductory period, each instructor was required to become a class coordinator and supervise a recruit class. The duty of directing your own class of recruits was highly valued at the training center. Most federal agencies delegated this role solely to supervisory individuals, but the Secret Service authorized nonsupervisory professionals to execute the task with the understanding that it taught and reinforced leadership skills for both students and trainers.

The pressure on educators was high, and there were no excuses if your class failed to meet the required requirements. Trainees would not hesitate to ruin your reputation in their assessments if you were not attentive and effective, which was a big motivator for the teaching team to produce a continuous, high-quality product. This encounter would teach me more about leadership than all my previous experiences combined. I rapidly realized that position and title do not make men or women effective leaders. My first few months with the students, many of whom were much older than myself, were turbulent. I went from wanting to be everyone's friend to becoming angry and frustrated when certain people took advantage of my nice nature. Learning the delicate balance between kindness and seeming vulnerability is not something that can be taught in a textbook.

Leadership in the real world is neither pretty nor glamorous, but it is extremely rewarding. Towards the end of the trainee program, I realized that leadership cannot be reduced to dazzling sound bites or a slogan on a sign. It takes the capacity to let people cry when they need to and tell them to stop sobbing when they don't. Being an effective leader entails being able to tell people you like that they are wrong and those you dislike that they are correct, and displaying your human flaws when a lesson needs to be taught. The class graduated from the Secret Service training facility with their heads held high, while I graduated from life's management school with a new perspective on how to lead and, more significantly, how not to.

Chapter 8: DIGNITARY PROTECTION AND THE FIGHT TO PROTECT

After three years of instructing and directing new recruits at the training center, I was relieved to learn that my chance to join the exclusive Presidential Protective Division was approaching. It is a little-known fact that only a small number of Secret Service agents advance to the president's protection detail. Protecting the president is the pinnacle of a Secret Service agent's career, and it is valued even more than a promotion. I worked hard to get to the point where I could be considered, and I still had one step to go before joining the elite PPD. Each agent was initially assigned to the Dignitary Protective Division (DPD) for a "trial run" before being chosen for either the president's or vice president's protection details.

This was a new requirement, and while it was the final step toward achieving my ultimate goal, it would add months, if not years, of additional protection time to my career, which I was not looking forward to. An agent's time on a protection detail, regardless of who the protectee is, is the most stressful part of his job. It entails traveling to extremely dangerous places of the world with little security for oneself, unusually early wake-up times, lengthy periods without eating, drinking, or access to restrooms, and living a life that revolves around the protector's schedule rather than your own. Furthermore, your family is making significant sacrifices, whether willingly or reluctantly. No family event is sacred in the Secret Service, and "luxuries" like attending your children's birthday parties or watching the delight in their eyes as they open gifts on Christmas mornings always take a back seat to your responsibilities.

There are other positions within the DPD, and I was quickly allocated to the operations branch. I was chosen for this post because of my expertise in the training center's operations division, and it was well known in the Secret Service that once you were identified as a competent "ops guy," it lasted with you. This was going to be different for me, however. The training center's operations section assigned me to manage scheduling and trainee matters rather than protection logistics. I had never been assigned to a full-time protective detail before and had no experience overseeing its operations. I began researching the job criteria and calling acquaintances for guidance. Protection details are distinct operational units with their own lexicon, regulations (both stated and implied), and standards of conduct, allowing agents to rapidly assess who is appropriate to be there and who is not. I was determined to fit in and not be a cautionary tale for other agents assigned to the section.

In the winter of 2005, I reported to the DPD operations unit during a midterm election and some staff changes in the Bush administration. These staff changes tended to have a significant influence on DPD agents. The agent's existence revolved around learning to predict and adapt to a protector's behavior, which can take years, and their replacement reset the entire cycle. Every time my phone called at the DPD, there was an issue that the caller wanted resolved "immediately," therefore I learnt to produce outcomes swiftly. I found myself tied to a phone and a desk for hours on end, calling our various field offices across the country and informing them that one of our protectees was on his way to their regions.

Many of the field offices I dealt with on a daily basis were located in high-traffic areas of the country for both protection and criminal investigations. Each visit by a DPD-managed protectee was an additional responsibility. Arrogance was a typical accusation directed against Secret Service operations agents, owing mostly to the fact that we issued instructions despite having no formal supervisory standing. Having never worked on a protective detail before, and being in charge of leading some of our seasoned field supervisors through the procedure of protection operations, was unsettling at times. I felt like I lacked credibility with them, but I did my best to help without coming across as arrogant, which some others struggled with.

We always had cable news stations on the office television in the DPD operations division to guarantee that we never missed a breaking news story. I'd listen to the news all day, which piqued my interest in political campaigns. I was particularly interested in the US Senate election in Maryland between former lieutenant governor Michael Steele and Representative Ben Cardin (my future political opponent). It was a political war in a blue state in an election year that promised to be historic for the Democratic Party. Steele's ability to remain competitive despite all the variables working against him amazed me, and I actively watched the election, hoping for a Maryland Republican triumph that never came.

The monotony of spending hours on the phone and computer, along with a lack of time in the field completing protection-related tasks, was draining my motivation. I had always taken pride in my operational competence, and manning a desk was eroding not only my talents but also my mental capacity. I asked DPD management if I might be briefly assigned to a protective detail to hone my security skills, and they agreed, assigning me to secure two international hotels for Department of Homeland Security Secretary Michael Chertoff. The first was the Imperial Hotel in Tokyo, Japan, while the second was the Shangri-La in Beijing, China.

Securing hotels to Secret Service standards is one of the most challenging things we do, and I was both excited and nervous about the prospect. Doing two consecutive security advances on the opposite side of the world as a reintroduction to operational advance work was a difficult task. I performed as much research on the two hotels as I could from my workstation at the DPD office, preparing for the lengthy journey.

When I arrived in Japan and started working on the task, I realized why hotels had always been so difficult. (Consider, for example, the

Ronald Reagan shooting at the Washington Hilton and the attempted assassination of President Gerald Ford outside the St. Francis Hotel in San Francisco.) Hotels are massive constructions built to keep people and equipment hidden from view. The cleaning and maintenance personnel take a roundabout route through concealed halls, allowing them to roam freely throughout the hotel while remaining out of sight of the visitors. This is an assassin's dream and a secret service agent's worst nightmare. We have an edge in any site where we are familiar with the geography, such as the White House, whereas hotel agents only have a limited amount of time to get as familiar with the countryside as they are with the White House.

The journey to the Imperial Hotel was taxing as I adjusted to the time shift and walked kilometers each day through its halls and up and down its stairwells. Secretary Chertoff's visit was pleasantly uneventful, and without a break, I boarded an aircraft to China. The relationship between the Secret Service and the staff at the Shangri-La in Beijing was extremely different from the one we had with the Imperial in Tokyo. The Imperial staff gave us unrestricted access to all aspects of the hotel, and they found it entertaining when we asked thorough inquiries. During our stay, we became familiar with the hotel's kitchens and back halls.

The security officers at the Shangri-La were more limited and cautious with our entry, which was consistent with the country's general skepticism about foreign security. They let me walk through the hotel, but I was stopped at every corner by a new security staff member and had to reaffirm my intentions at every turn. It was simultaneously irritating and impressive. The tight security added hours to what should have been a relatively simple advance at the Shangri-La, but it would serve me well during the visit, and I was confident in their abilities to regulate access to the hotel sections we were most concerned about. I reasoned that if I couldn't get along a hallway without being faced by every landscape element, neither could a hypothetical assassin.

The tour was a success, but more importantly for me, it served as a crash lesson in protection, preparing me for my next duty with the Presidential Protective Division.

Chapter 9: THE "BIG SHOW": THE PRESIDENTIAL PROTECTIVE DIVISION

Every Secret Service agent's first day in the White House as a PPD member is a surreal experience. Walking through the claustrophobia-inducing hallways of the West Wing and stumbling into the nation's most powerful men and women is something most people can only picture from television. However, I was quickly immersed in the actual security workings of the president's detail, with little opportunity to ponder on my surroundings.

To eliminate hesitancy, Secret Service personnel from the PPD are continually rehearsing complex solutions to any probable scenario that requires action. Because of this, the Secret Service was hesitant to send new agents to the PPD outside the White House grounds until they had gained some experience with the detail's internal dynamics; thus, I knew I'd have the opportunity to process security protocol inside the White House before being asked to take on more responsibility. Presidential security is such a difficult operation with so many variables that I had to be careful not to get ahead of myself and instead focus on doing the job at hand each day to the best of my ability.

In addition to memorizing infinite security plans, new PPD agents were required to understand a set of unwritten regulations. Mastering the unwritten rules was just as difficult as learning the written ones, and the consequences for breaking them were harsh. One of the unbreakable laws was never to be caught on the White House grounds dressed in anything other than business clothing, unless it was the dress code for the day (for example, golf with the president). Breaking this rule resulted in a succession of bad assignments, therefore it was usually a one-time mistake. Another unwritten rule was to never approach the protectee in an uninvited chat. Any agent who couldn't resist the impulse to initiate a conversation with the president would have his time on the detail cut short.

After a two-month period working on President George W. Bush's shift and experiencing the intense heat at his Waco ranch, the difficulties of changing from a suit to ranch attire in the bathroom of Air Force One, learning how to open the doors of the presidential limo (it is not easy), constantly battling for parking on the White House grounds, and the zero tolerance for whining and complaining, the indoctrination process was completed, and I was promptly transferred to the

As part of their PPD career path, all new agents were required to complete an assignment on one of the Bush daughters' details following a two-month assignment on the presidential shift. These minor things are less controlled, and building personal relationships with the protectees, while frowned upon, is not unusual. I found Jenna to be affable, kind, and extremely adventurous, and I learned from agents that she had an intense travel schedule planned for the next year—a fact my wife found disturbing, as Paula had grown accustomed to my consistent work hours and lighter travel load during my time in the DPD and at the training center. Jenna's routine revolved around a book she was writing about her experiences with an HIV-positive lady named Ana while working for UNICEF. We intended to travel to South America for a prolonged visit shortly after my arrival, following a road trip across the United States she had planned.

Working as an agent on Jenna's detail was fascinating because the security footprint was effective but less visible than the president's. This absence of apparent security would elicit the same bewildered reaction from those who recognized her. They would spot her and then search the area for the Secret Service. When they didn't immediately see us, I could read their lips as they said, "That's not her." Following her in the vehicles on her cross-country trip became a game, as the agent I was assigned to partner with, Matt, and I would watch the passing vehicles do this repeatedly.

During my first few weeks with Jenna, I appreciated the change of pace. Not having to fight for parking on the White House lawn or wear a business suit every day considerably reduced my stress level. We were always on the move, and each day brought a new experience. Finding hotels to stay in throughout the road trip became a daily adventure as we drove through small towns in America that most people will never see or even hear about. Our two-week journey concluded at Bandon, Oregon, a hamlet that appeared pleasantly astonished by our arrival in their peaceful corner of America. With a population of just over 3,000, the entrance of the first daughter and a cadre of Secret Service personnel provoked both excitement and bewilderment, with some questioning whether it was Jenna Bush. When we stepped into a local restaurant, it felt like a scene from a movie, with the jukebox going silent and everyone's attention drawn to the front door. The townspeople were either happy or surprised that we were there—in any case, they treated us well, and the excitement we had created in town was palpable, as everyone we passed seemed to know who we were and gave us a not-so-subtle wink or nod. This exciting cross-country trip was only a foretaste of our approaching South American adventure.

Jenna's South American tour began with a visit to Panama. The agents and I intended to spend a lengthy period of time in Panama City, and considering the duration of the trip, we needed to plan accordingly. Items that we take for granted in our daily lives become problematic when living abroad in a hotel that is not built for long-term inhabitants. Finding food, clean water, a gym, and adequate medical care (which would become vital for me shortly after arrival) were continual obstacles.

Fortunately, our Panamanian security counterparts made these jobs seem less onerous. They were assigned to us 24 hours a day and could perform almost anything. They appeared to be connected to a network of insiders who could obtain anything we required. Throughout my employment, I discovered that this tendency is extremely common internationally. We in the United States have a government that allows us to live without fear of police enforcement. This is not true in many other countries. I found that a history of government persecution or internal warfare instilled distrust of law enforcement in many of these countries' populations. One Panamanian told me, "Those who have the guns, have the power." This authority gives law enforcement officers access to an influential network of people whose status does not necessarily match their own.

After a few days of acclimating to the water and environment while waiting for Jenna to join the team, I suffered the normal gastrointestinal bug that plagued almost every overseas vacation I took. However, further issues arose shortly after her arrival. The agents on Jenna's detail had grown accustomed to the quirks of operating on a smaller, less regulated detail with a daring protectee. We knew her tendencies and how to communicate with her, but PPD management decided to send an Assistant Special Agent in Charge (ASAIC) down to Panama with us to handle the operation, despite his lack of expertise working with Jenna. Conflicts over the implementation of our protection plan did not take long to develop.

We had established some innovative yet effective unorthodox techniques to keep Jenna safe, and the agents on the detail and I were frustrated by the ASAIC's constant second-guessing given our track record of success up to that time. After a week of internal fighting, one agent in particular, who had an excellent reputation for honesty, became dissatisfied and questioned the ASAIC. The ASAIC was taken aback when the subordinate agent addressed him strongly. We won the exchange, and the ASAIC promptly left the nation, much to the relief of the detail and Jenna.

Being a Secret Service agent on a foreign protection mission entails more than just tactical risks. Before traveling to Panama, I, along with the rest of Jenna's details, were warned about the various illnesses we may contract in South America if we were not careful. Malaria was still a problem, and the White House Medical Unit strongly recommended us to dress appropriately and generously apply mosquito repellent. I ignored the advice despite having traveled with the Secret Service for years and never encountered anything worse than normal stomach diseases. It was a decision I would later regret.

I was assigned to work the afternoon shift on February 4, 2007, Super Bowl Sunday, with Andrew, the agent who had received me at the White House during my first shift. Jenna was not planning to leave her modest apartment, so we anticipated a quiet night. We lived in the flat just next door, and we had a little television with a picture so bad you couldn't recognize a face on it. Between shifts watching the apartment, we could watch the Colts and Bears compete for the Super Bowl championship.

During the night, I started feeling ill, but unlike a typical cold or flu, which usually creeps on slowly, I was deteriorating quickly, and within thirty minutes, I felt like I was about to pass out. Mike, the acting supervisor on the trip and a personal buddy from my days at the New York and Melville offices, was concerned and swiftly dispatched another agent to the apartment to relieve me so I could return to the hotel. What followed was the most agonizing experience I'd ever had.

I had contracted dengue fever through a mosquito bite. The symptoms I experienced helped me understand why the condition is sometimes known as "break-bone fever." I was in and out of consciousness all night, alone at the hotel, feeling as if my entire body was being crushed while fluctuating between high fever and bone-chilling shivering. I was sweating intensely and had drenched the mattress I was lying on, leaving me badly dehydrated.

When the sun came up and I realized how serious my position was, I called Mike and explained what was going on. He immediately called our Miami field office, which had control over the South American region, and begged for assistance. Mike also instructed Tom to pick me up and drive me to a local medical institution that was hopelessly out of line with American medical norms. Working with the Miami field office, Mike scheduled a trip and had Miami agents meet me at the airport to guarantee I caught my connecting flight home. My illness worsened on the flight, and by the time I arrived home, I had lost about fifteen pounds of fluids. Paula picked me up from the airport and looked after me. I didn't return to work for three weeks, and it took another month to go back to my regular physical state.

Although the infectious disease specialist I was visiting to deal with the consequences of acquiring dengue fever urged me not to return to work, after three weeks I became restless. The physician also told me that dengue fever can be contracted again after infection, and the second time can be fatal. She informed me that dengue hemorrhagic fever, which causes serious internal bleeding, is probable with a subsequent infection, and that I should avoid returning to South America.

I ignored the specialist and contacted PPD operations and Mike, telling them to put me back on the operational shift. Jenna had already left Panama and was on her way to Argentina with the detail, and I felt as if I would be failing the team if I stayed behind on sick leave. We were a minor detail, and the loss of one agent just meant that everyone else had to pick up the load. On PPD, we never allow illness reduce our security footprint. If someone felt unwell, someone else on the detail had to fill in, tripling his working hours. I determined that, despite my fragile condition, I needed to return to work. I resumed a rigorous workout routine to physically prepare myself and dedicated to regaining full fitness before leaving for Argentina.

Argentina presented the same set of difficulties as Panama in terms of food, water, and housing accommodations. It would be another long vacation. One significant difference between the two countries was that Argentina would create significant security issues, as opposed to Panama, which would be rather unremarkable. We had been in a very controlled atmosphere in Panama because of the security measures in place where we stayed with Jenna. (The presence of a United Nations office within our Panamanian building provided some welcome extra security.) We didn't have such luxury in Argentina. Jenna chose an apartment along a public street in a district of Buenos Aires with a high crime rate, so we would have to make adjustments.

The crime problem became apparent within a few days when a Miami agent on a temporary assignment to assist us reported over the radio that a man was assaulting his girlfriend in front of Jenna's apartment and had drawn a knife. These incidents were not unusual on the street where the apartment was located, but they lessened significantly as the residents figured out who we were and why we were there. The street-crime situation in other parts of Argentina, on the other hand, was about to disgrace the Secret Service when Jenna's sister, Barbara, decided to pay us a visit and we became the subject of the story.

Despite increased security due to the presence of both of the president's daughters in the country, Barbara's purse was stolen while she was sipping coffee at an outdoor café on her first day in Buenos Aires, presumably from the back of the chair. I was working with Jenna, not Barbara, on the day of the incident, but I was not far from the area, and neither I nor the other agents remembered seeing anything peculiar. Our security operation is solely concerned with protecting people, not their stuff, so when Barbara reported that she was missing her purse, we thought that she may have walked away from it, and while our attention was focused on her rather than her bag, someone snatched it.

Our experiences with Jenna Bush continued as we journeyed through South America and beyond. The first daughter was scheduled for a quick trip to Kingston, Jamaica, where we were to meet with ABC's Diane Sawyer to do a profile of Jenna and talk about her impending book. Diane and Jenna planned to film a scene where they were strolling down an alleyway in inner Kingston. We had to guard the area while they spoke and the camera crew filmed. It wasn't long before the area became overcrowded with residents, both interested and suspicious.

At the time, Kingston was the world's homicide capital, and we weren't going to add to that dire figure. Still, the security situation deteriorated rapidly. Some of the locals were plainly armed, and we were immediately surrounded at the end of the alley, with just one way out. We decided to conclude the session right once and rushed Jenna and Diane to an armored SUV that was waiting for us.

Surprisingly, the ABC camera crew appeared unaffected by what had just happened. One of the cameramen I spoke with about the incident later that night told me that he was in Somalia in the days leading up to the Black Hawk Down incident and learnt to just keep filming no matter what. His resolve amazed me. When the film emerged as part of an ABC 20/20 documentary months later, the agents' frustration and worry of failing in our goal to keep our protectee safe was palpable.

As my time on Jenna's detail came to an end, I was invited to consider which assignment I preferred next. As part of the PPD career path, the next step would be one of three distinct "satellites," as they were referred to inside the detail. My options included the first lady's bodyguard detail, the transportation division, or the counter surveillance unit. While each assignment had merits and cons, it was universally acknowledged that the transportation division had the most diverse set of tasks and required logistics ability, which would be useful in any future Secret Service assignment. I was apprehensive to request the task at first, and I considered the first lady's detail, but after the purse snatching incident, dengue infection, and near-death experience in Kingston, I decided it was time to go on to the next step. I joined the transportation sector, eager to begin anew.

Chapter 10: TRANSPORTATION: IT'S NOT SIMPLY ABOUT MOTORCADES

The Transportation Section marked a dramatic shift in operating tempo from Jenna's detail. Our growing triumphs went mostly unnoticed, while our failures were continual fuel, primarily for agents on the more glamorous first lady's detail. As a result, the transportation division tended to attract type A personalities who sought a high-risk, no-reward work environment. It was generally known that, despite the enormous amount of effort put into developing safe and efficient motorcade routes, we were rarely congratulated for transporting the president from A to B. Furthermore, driving the president's limousine is one of the most demanding tasks. The media usually refers to the limo as "the Beast," despite transportation agents never using this absurd term and can separate media people "in the know" from those attempting to appear as if they are simply by whether or not they use that term.

While driving an unwieldy armored limousine, the agent must be prepared to take one of the alternate motorcade routes at any time, as well as be familiar with all of the relocation points and safe zones, all while attempting to avoid rear-ending the car in front of him and then answering questions from the detail supervisor and the president. Although the practice is usually error-free, hiccups are not unusual, and with the White House press corps always there, they are always recorded for the world to see. Some of the more famous footage, recorded on YouTube, involves one of our presidential limousines halting on a street in Italy packed with people, as well as one of the limousines colliding with a security gate that failed to descend in Ireland, stranding the entire convoy in its wake.

Despite thousands of uneventful motorcades due to the preparedness and dedication of the transportation section's men and women, these public failures have served as cautionary tales to rookie agents. Even if the actual security implications are minor, Secret Service headquarters fears public embarrassment, and with a limited public relations machine (unlike the FBI, which has more manpower and thus greater ability to handle public relations), they frequently make an example of agents who they hold accountable for high-profile failures. This would come to haunt any agent involved in the terrible 2012 Colombian prostitute scandal.

With the penalties of failure constantly on my mind, I dedicated myself completely to studying the intricacies of conducting transportation breakthroughs for the president. The transportation branch, like everything else on the PPD, brought their agents along slowly and assigned easier tasks to the newer agents first. They also guaranteed that a more experienced agent from the section walked the novice agents through the complex planning process.

My first advance was referred to as "in-town." This was the word used to designate a motorcade that stayed entirely within the confines of Washington, DC. Although the planning was intensive, the journeys were easier logistically and were generally the first assignments for new agents. In-towns were often done with both Secret Service personnel and law enforcement agencies who were well-versed in the PPD's operational needs and could handle the task without any coaching. Although my first excursion was in-town, it was a long one to Walter Reed Hospital. The path to the hospital was just inside the limitations for driving rather than utilizing the presidential helicopter, Marine One, and would necessitate a large number of police personnel to assure a safe and secure journey.

In preparation, I traveled the intended motorcade route nonstop, familiarizing myself with every nook and cranny on the road and in the surrounding area. After days of planning and preparing for contingencies, I was eager for "game day," as Secret Service personnel refer to the day of the presidential visit. When I went out of the White House's Diplomatic Reception Room and didn't know the officer in charge of driving the lead police vehicle, I knew there was a problem. My fears were verified when, only a few minutes into the twenty-minute drive, he grabbed a paper copy of the route from the console, jammed it against the steering wheel, and began rapidly flipping through the pages. I saw he didn't know where he was going, so I told him to put the paperwork down and I'd show him the way. The sense of relief when we got to Walter Reed was indescribable. I was silently grateful that I had driven the road frequently enough to navigate it almost blindly. During the advance, I was helped by Tim, a coworker and buddy from the training center who had arrived in the transportation area a few weeks earlier and was still calling me "Big City." Tim was a quick learner who warned me not to rely on others to know the motorcade route, which clearly paid off on this specific occasion.

Following the successful planning and implementation of the Walter Reed Hospital in-town visit, I was assigned to Lancaster, Pennsylvania, for my first out-of-town mission. The small distance from the Washington metropolitan area would make the trip more manageable. Visits near Washington, DC, like this one, allowed us to travel to the places utilizing Secret Service vehicles, eliminating the need to fly and rent a car.

We departed Washington and arrived in Lancaster just a few hours later, checked into our hotel, and got ready to work. The first step in any trip outside Washington is a police meeting that brings together all local police agencies and emergency workers. All of the agents (including the transportation agent) deliver extensive briefings on what we do and what we require from them. This was the first police meeting where I would be presenting material. As I sat in the room waiting for the meeting to begin, I remembered my first police meeting when I was assigned to the Melville office. Scott from the Hillary Clinton detail had delivered a slick and professional brief that earned him instant respect from the police officers, and the recollection weighed heavily on me. I discreetly rehearsed my presentation to ensure that I remembered everything correctly, and when it was my turn to speak, I did so with confidence.

After the discussion, I met privately with select supervisory police personnel and the Secret Service lead advance and requested that they inform PPD operations that we will use Marine One to fly rather than drive to the first Lancaster site on the timetable. I believed that a Marine One helicopter lift would cause minimum disturbance to traffic patterns and allow President Bush to land directly across the street from the plant we were inspecting. My concerns were addressed, but I was informed that because of logistics issues, we would have to use armored cars to drive from the airport to the Lancaster site.

On the day of the visit, as we drove the president from the landing zone to the factory, I saw traffic backing up quickly on the other side of the road. As the convoy moved forward, the traffic situation deteriorated substantially. We were all vividly aware that President Bush saw what we all saw: a mile-long traffic jam. The president insisted on causing as little disruption as possible to the inhabitants of the communities he selected to visit.

A few months later, I was sent to the White House and had the opportunity to see an event that few people see from the inside but many from the outside. An Oval Office speech is usually reserved for the most somber of presidential addresses. It is a technique that is utilized seldom, and when it is, the beauty of the office serves to enhance and repeat the message. Almost everyone in my generation remembers Ronald Reagan's Oval Office address following the Challenger disaster. His powerful address helped console a bereaved nation.

In September 2007, I stood outside the thick white door to the Oval Office and watched President George W. Bush address the world from the legendary Oval Office desk, made of wood from the British explorer ship Resolute, about the War on Terror in Iraq. After over a decade of serving in the White House and for the Secret Service, there were only a few occasions that truly captivated my emotions. But standing there, a city kid who grew up above a bar eating Cheerios for dinner, staring straight at the president of the United States as he addressed hundreds of millions of people about a watershed point in our history, was a particularly moving experience in my life.

The stress of working in the transportation department is heightened around the end of a president's second term. Presidents frequently conduct overseas "farewell tours" as their terms in office draw to an end, and these excursions are extremely labor-intensive from a security standpoint. Collaboration and planning with foreign security, police, and military professionals differs significantly from organizing a visit with state or municipal emergency authorities in the United States. In some foreign countries, personnel standards and training levels, and equipment preparedness, differ significantly from those in the United States. When executing a security advance for the president in a foreign country, queries like "Is this bridge structurally stable?" are usual. It makes no sense to secure a motorcade route if the roads and infrastructure cannot support the weight of the presidential limousine and may collapse when we drive over them. Driving in foreign nations can also be dangerous due to the sometimes chaotic and disorganized traffic patterns, which we are not used to in the United States.

The Lost City of Petra was carved into the stone walls of deep cliffs in the Jordanian desert. The intricacy in the massive structures is stunning. This astounding feat in preindustrial engineering was also immortalized as the mythical Canyon of the Crescent Moon in the film Indiana Jones and the Last Crusade.

Clearance to navigate our armored vehicles through the Siq, a long passage dug deep into the cavern, was a source of dispute for the Jordanians, who preferred that no vehicles be allowed on this sacred site. However, given the high threat level of the visit, I could not allow the first lady to travel such a long distance without access to an armored vehicle for evacuation. On this journey, there was a real fear of a concerted attack on the convoy on Petra's razor-thin roads by area extremists.

After a week of negotiations between myself, the Secret Service's main advance agent, John, and the French, they agreed to our request to close the Champs Élysées, which resolved one issue. But the security of the bike trip remained an unanswered issue. I instructed an advance team agent named Frank to select a place for the bike ride and devise a strategy to obtain it. He assured me that the route he eventually chose was secure, and we were content with our plan. During the outing, our confidence rapidly turned to panic when the president rode off the designated bike route at his usual fast pace, and we struggled to maintain visual contact with him from the road. My heart rate increased swiftly as I thought to myself, "Please do not lose the President."

Chapter 11: THE PRESIDENT'S LIFE IN MY HANDS

After years of diligently working through the Secret Service ranks to be selected for the Presidential Protective Division, I discovered that there is no competitive break after you arrive there. A tiny number of agents are chosen for the PPD, and even fewer are chosen as lead advance agents for the president, the pinnacle of operational excellence. One mistake and your chances of being selected as a lead advance agent are over. Unlike many top-heavy departments in our federal government, the Secret Service maintains a flat management structure and delegates a significant amount of responsibility to its detail agents. Lead advance agents are solely responsible for the overall security plan and, ultimately, ensuring the president's safety during any visit outside of the White House premises. Managing an entire advance team, overseeing the security budget, and serving as the face of the White House alongside White House officials is an honor and a pleasure, and I was determined to surpass expectations.

President-elect Obama's inauguration was going to necessitate a complex security plan, and I was pleased to play a key part in its execution. The Secret Service and the Presidential Inaugural Committee (PIC) were aware that this would be a historic event with an unparalleled turnout. The law enforcement and military resources devoted to protecting this event were unparalleled. Law enforcement officers were brought in from all around the country, while military soldiers from specialist teams were sent to crucial places in Washington, DC.

Although the security operation we prepared was excellent, I could see the PPD management team's concern in their eyes as I briefed them in a secure room situated in a dark part of the White House complex's eighteen acres. It was not a look I was accustomed to. Everyone in the room knew the president was going to leave the safety of our tank-like armored presidential limousine and walk the parade route, despite any reservations we might have had, and the fears were valid. Securing an entire street in Washington, DC, and ensuring the same degree of protection as the White House grounds is a massive security endeavor, and if even one weapon managed to slip into our protected zone, a historic disaster was almost certain.

Despite my fervent support for Senator John McCain during the election, I felt proud of my country that day. A presidential inauguration is not the time to choose a political brawl. I heard the newly inaugurated president's address blaring from speakers positioned throughout the city and watched as many individuals in the audience began to cry. Some of those people did not need to learn about the civil rights era in textbooks; they had experienced the pain and indignity of that age, and while the wounds may heal, the scars will remain. Witnessing the pleasure in their eyes as they stood in the severe cold, listening to the words of our first African American president, is something I will never forget.

It also influenced me politically. I came to the unpleasant understanding that my political party had done a terrible job of addressing the long-term scars caused by this dark chapter in our collective American history, and relaying the message about their critical role in ending it. Fortunately, most of us will never face the humiliation of institutional racism, but as a nation, we must never forget that the power of government has not always been a store of good intentions.

The assignment that followed President Obama's first inauguration was not as momentous, but the president's safety is not dependent on any history lesson. As part of his endeavor to grow in the role, the president had booked a number of outings outside the White House grounds following his inauguration, one of which I was to participate in.

When I received a phone call from the operations section about a presidential visit to Trinidad, I knew it was too early for me to conduct the lead advance, but I was pleasantly delighted to be chosen to handle the security advance for the Hilton Hotel that the staff had chosen for the trip. The Secret Service regarded this hotel as exceedingly difficult to safeguard due to its intricate layout. It was generally known as the "Upside-Down Hilton."

Pete, the White House photographer, captured an official shot of the president entering the car, which shows me staring up and loudly telling a guest to close his hotel window. I was sent the photo, and when I look at it, I recall how bad I felt.

Completing the Trinidad Hilton advance allowed me to mark a task off my fictional career "to-do" list. The Secret Service is a fantastic organization that instills in its agents a commitment to the goal that greatly outweighs financial compensation. Imagine a private company asking its employees to take on a responsibility equivalent to securing the life of the President of the United States, to work ten to sixteen hours per day without a day off in a foreign country where your life is constantly in danger, and to do so for no additional compensation. This is the life of a PPD lead advance agent working on an international advance in a high-threat country. Despite these circumstances, PPD operatives yearn for the possibility to be sent to a foreign advance, and the more perilous the better. I applaud the Secret Service for creating, whether consciously or not, a culture in which your credibility as an agent is dependent on taking on increasing levels of responsibility and rewarding agents who complete the most challenging assignments. The benefits are not material, but rather based on group dynamics and social status inside the detail. After selecting the international hotel advance box, I was eager to move on to lead advance work and was pleased to be assigned to my first post at a Caterpillar facility in Youngstown, Ohio.

It was also during this trip that I had a life-changing talk with an older, more experienced agent whom I considered a mentor. Ken and I had quickly become friends on the PPD, where he had been assigned as a supervisor, and his participation in the Youngstown trip was a bonus. Ken, like Steve, the agent I worked with on the Trinidad trip, always had wise advice to provide, information gleaned from life experience, work experience, and a good sense of when to speak and when to listen. Ken had been assigned to a number of high-profile jobs, including a lengthy term on Capitol Hill in a renowned senator's office, and his experiences had shaped him, both positively and negatively.

Although I enjoyed my time with the Secret Service and would not have given the rich experiences and close, personal ties with some of my fellow agents for anything, there was something missing. Ken felt my concern, and after a day of difficult advance work in Youngstown, I informed him that I was considering quitting. I didn't know why at the time, but I told him I felt compelled to make a difference in the world and wasn't sure whether this was the way to do so. Ken, a genuinely religious but not preachy gentleman, encouraged me to pray about it and seek spiritual guidance. He made it plain that you needed to ask for help and that the answers would be obvious, but only if you had the courage to take the test. Following this conversation, the concept of politics entered my conscious mind.

During our visit, the Paspampres were led by General Marciano Norman, the current head of the Indonesian State Intelligence Agency, who was physically impressive and spoke loudly. Norman was close to Indonesian President Susilo Bambang Yudhoyono (remember my lesson from Panama that in some countries, "those who have the guns have the power"), and maintaining a good relationship with him was going to be critical to the mission's success, whereas one wrong calculation with Norman could jeopardize the visit's success. Norman could fix almost anything if we wanted him to, and when he talked, it was evident he was speaking on behalf of the Indonesian president. My relationship with Norman, while delicate, aided in the removal of a number of bureaucratic roadblocks, which always influenced the pace of any overseas advance. I rapidly learned to stage my requests, gradually preparing him for what would undoubtedly be an unparalleled demand for intelligence assets, equipment, manpower, and traffic control.

Throughout the advance, I was constantly concerned about the potential of terrorism and the team's personal safety. The Secret Service protects the president, but the Secret Service does not enjoy the same privileges. Force protection became a top issue for me, and I met with Jakarta Shangri-La staff on a daily basis to learn what they were doing to prevent another bombing like the one that occurred at the JW Marriott in South Jakarta in 2003. I couldn't explain to the family of a fellow Secret Service agent that I lost him or her to an attack because we were so preoccupied with the president's protection that we neglected our own.

I was unhappy that the White House personnel in Indonesia had not told me sooner. International discussions and diplomacy are always sensitive. I was certain that General Norman would believe that I had withheld this information from him and that the White House personnel in Indonesia had been aware of the cancellation in advance. I hastily grabbed the nearest phone in an effort to keep Norman from hearing about the cancellation on the news, and dialed his assistant Frega's number. I apologized politely and praised Frega for his efforts to ensure a safe visit. Frega, a fine man, said he understood and promised me that there would be no ill will with Norman.

Chapter 12: MISSILE TREATIES AND THE RETURN TO INDONESIA

I chose to use some of my collected vacation time to spend time with Paula and our daughter, Isabel, after making the long journey home from Indonesia, genuinely saddened at the wasted effort put in by me and the team. She assumed my wife and I had separated. Hearing that was emotionally distressing. I'd missed so many birthdays and holidays, and they are memories that, once lost, cannot be recovered. Paula was understanding, but she was also frustrated. Excited about the break from the daily grind, I drove into PPD operations to drop off the secure phones and diplomatic passports assigned to the Indonesia advance team, intending to leave the office immediately to return home and begin my vacation. Unfortunately it was not.

When I stepped into the White House compound, Marlon, the operations supervisor, asked whether I was ready to go out again. Confused, I asked what he meant. He told me that the White House was nearing the finish of negotiations for the START II deal, and that depending on the outcome of the talks, the president might travel to Prague to sign the pact with Russian President Dmitry Medvedev.

After spending some time at home with my family and keeping busy with advance work in the United States, I became concerned about the state of the country and my role in it. I witnessed a voyage down an economic road our government had previously attempted with devastating outcomes, and as a result, my academic interest in economics grew into a passion. I read huge quantities of information on Austrian School economic theory whenever I had free time, whether on aircraft or at lunch. It inspired my growing enthusiasm for political activism. It appeared that the only thing that could keep me out of politics was an advance assignment, but given my recent work in Prague and Indonesia, I didn't anticipate another major assignment in the near future. My expectations for my workload could not have been more out of line with what was to follow.

In June 2010, I received a phone call from PPD operations, asking how I felt about Indonesia. Confused, I replied that I had a great time there and was disappointed that the visit had been canceled. I was informed that the visit was now officially resumed, and that PPD management wanted me to return to Indonesia to repeat the advance based on my previous experience there. I knew this would cause some concern among the PPD lead advance agents because these key assignments were becoming increasingly difficult to come by, given the president's limited travel schedule due to the Obamacare discussions and the now-erupting BP oil leak disaster.

I was stunned. This was the second time we'd cancelled, and I was aware of how much diplomatic currency had already been spent on the trip. Personally, I thought it would be impossible to maintain any credibility with General Norman in Indonesia. He had already set aside thousands of man-hours for this, and now I'd have to call Frega and inform him that the trip had been canceled again.

Chapter 13: OIL SPILLS, INDONESIA AGAIN, AND MAKING A WAR ZONE "SAFE"

Arriving home AFTER THE SECOND CANCELLATION of the Indonesia trip, I concluded that my time with the details was coming to an end, and the trip was simply not meant to be. I despised the fact that we worked so hard on a strategy that would never be implemented, while our international law-enforcement relationships with the Indonesians deteriorated.

I hadn't been home for more than a few hours when PPD operations contacted to ask if I could assist another agent with his first lead advance assignment. The agent was Tim, a good buddy from our time at the training center and the PPD transportation department. I was proud to do it, and while Paula was disappointed that I had to leave again, she and Tim were friends, and she knew what had to be done. Tim and I were sent to Dauphin Island, Alabama, with the president to look for evidence of an oil leak. The White House staff looked to be trying to make the president appear to be "doing something" and wanted some photos of him on an oily beach appearing concerned. The general public can see through this, but every presidential administration I've worked for has adopted this tactic, no matter how plainly choreographed it appears.

My positive perspective immediately evaporated when I heard whispers inside the detail that the Indonesia trip was being considered again among White House officials. Paula would not agree to my coming to Indonesia for a third prospective presidential visit with a similar timetable. The hazards would now be amplified since any group wishing to harm the president would have months to prepare. Although no one from PPD operations confirmed any plans with me, I felt confident that I would be invited to return again. I gradually prepared Paula for the inevitable phone call from operations, and just a few days later, I found myself on the long journey back to Indonesia for the third time.

According to some of my pals who were detailed there, the India leg of the trip was a "disaster," and the PPD administration was not in the mood for any more mistakes. The Indian security force assigned to the visit had broken promises made during the advance and openly disobeyed the Secret Service advance team's desires, resulting in an embarrassing situation for both the Secret Service and its staff. Patience had worn thin, and I knew our visit had to be perfect.

The fun began when a security representative from the hotel where the president would be staying ran up to me with a troubled expression on his face and a picture in his palm. He added that a man had checked into various rooms at the hotel under different names and traveled back and forth between them before leaving. The Indonesians confirmed for us that the man was affiliated with a variety of groups, which concerned both me and the intelligence agents on the ground.

When the sweep returned negative findings, I was mildly relieved, but I began to worry if all of this poor luck was a sign that the trip was doomed. Suffering from a chronic lack of sleep and feeling exceedingly uncomfortable wearing suffocating gear in near-hundred-degree temperatures, I prepared our motorcade and drove to the airport to eventually pick up the president.

The Indonesia vacation, which had been officially cut short owing to ash plumes from the erupting volcano, was moving well as we proceeded from the airport to the hotel and then to the Indonesian presidential palace. The security plan we devised was operating flawlessly, but the ash plumes were thickening, and the White House Military Office became increasingly alarmed. The next morning, I met with the PPD advance team and the supervisors assigned to the visit. They informed me that to shorten the visit by a few hours, we would cancel the last scheduled stop and travel directly from a speech at a nearby university to the airport.

It was becoming a race against the clock to avoid the exploding volcano and rising ash plume. Our first destination of the day, the Istiqlal Mosque, was hasty as we made our way to the speech venue. Despite the reduced schedule, the president was greeted with a hero's welcome on campus. We still hadn't found the strange man at the hotel, and with the ash plume approaching, I was relieved to see the president leave the country sooner than expected. Coordinating the logistics of the early departure was made slightly more difficult because the president was not returning to the United States but flying immediately to South Korea, which was not prepared to greet him.

I contacted Colin, the lead advance in South Korea, and informed him that he needed to meet with the South Koreans to change the schedule. Meanwhile, during the procession from the university to the airport, I quietly prayed that the security arrangement would hold and that we would safely transport the president. The stress was increasing, and when mixed with crushing exhaustion and the scorching Indonesian heat, I dreaded the worse. Between the suspicious hotel guests, the indigenous threats I encountered on a daily basis, and the ash cloud that threatened to strand the president in Indonesia if we fell even a few minutes behind schedule, I was constantly on the phone with new requests for the crew.

A few days into my journey, I met with General David Petraeus, the commander of the International Security Assistance Force, in downtown Kabul after flying from Bagram in the rear of a war-torn C-130 cargo jet. Our visit with the general was excellent. I found him to be extremely open to our ideas, and I was honored that, given his expertise in the country, he was willing to hear and adopt my suggestions for how we could assure the president's safety in this unusual situation. We reviewed several transportation alternatives for the president if he decides to travel to Kabul, and while the general told me that transportation could be obtained, I was hesitant to approve them. This became a difficult issue, with wildly differing perspectives on it. General Petraeus believed it could be done, but several of his colleagues disagreed, and intelligence officers on the ground strongly warned against it. They believed that if we were detected, we would be shot out of the sky by rocket-propelled grenade fire as we left Kabul. I trust scouts in the field. They worked in highly difficult situations, and unfortunately, two years later, the location where I visited with them was attacked with heavy weaponry, killing two heroes.

The decision to allow the president to fly to Kabul from Bagram would be a watershed event for me. After speaking with Ambassador Karl Eikenberry at our mission in Kabul, I remained unconvinced that the trip could be secured. I knew we could easily secure the airstrip at Bagram, but downtown Kabul was unlike anything I'd ever seen. It appeared that time had forgotten certain parts of the city, and law and order were nonexistent. We travelled with heavily armed troops and did not leave the US facility without heavily armored jackets and windowless armored vehicles.

My wife emailed me, finally figuring out what my mysterious mission had been. Her texts were urgent, and she was naturally frightened for my safety. The scenario was one of controlled pandemonium, and the lack of light on the airstrip made it difficult to see anything other than the flashing flashes of White House press pool photographers. We needed to keep the lights low to avoid being a target for enemy mortar fire. I used my flashlight to safeguard the president from stumbling on the runway.

The first visit was the troop rally. Although it was late at night local time, the attendees were very welcoming. We worked away from the president while he slowly shook every hand in the crowd, taking almost an hour to greet each soldier. As time passed, I became increasingly anxious about our security situation. I knew our opponents were now aware that the president was on the ground, and with each passing minute, the danger increased. I was also receiving minute-by-minute updates on the situation of our stranded soldiers in Kabul. We really needed them to get in the air and head to Bagram.

My next stop with the president was the base hospital, where he would present Purple Hearts to the injured heroes on the premises. I kept my distance from the president as he chatted with the soldiers to respect their privacy, and I witnessed the men' faces light up as he took time with each of them. After five years on the PPD, I was ready to move on, but instances like these always rekindled my enthusiasm for my job.

As the night progressed, I became increasingly exhausted. It was an enormous relief to receive a phone call from the Kabul crew informing me that a brief opening had opened and that, while risky, they would be able to fly and land in Bagram with just enough time to make their flight home. The conference with the soldiers was long and I knew we still had several hours before the task was completed. The final logistics were set up. Air Force One would take off without runway lights to prevent being hit by mortar fire, but the lights would be turned on for the support plane carrying me and my team. As a result, to lessen our chances of being shot down by mortars, we had to take off right after Air Force One. To speed up the departure, I asked all of the support people we could spare without jeopardizing security to board the plane.

As the president completed his visit, I made sure he said his closing comments inside the hangar rather than on the runway. We would be finished with the visit after this final meeting, but not before a brief moment of inadvertent laughter. President Obama was supposed to meet with a small group of military leaders and a Delta Force operator, who was patiently standing outside the conference room wearing all of his equipment, including his guns. A staff member approached me and asked if I would mind notifying the Delta Force operator to turn in his weapons before entering the room. Tired and in no mood for idiocy, I laughed out loud at this preposterous request, considering that we had deployed every armed military unit on the base to assist us secure the president, and now he wanted me to ask an elite member of one of the best military forces the world has ever seen to drop his weapon. This brief interaction exemplified the insulated, out-of-touch world in which some Washington, DC cocktail party attendees operate. One single look into the Delta Force operator's eyes was enough to tell his story, one that never ends happily but always has a hero.

Chapter 14: MEDIA SPIN VS. SECURITY REALITY

A DISTURBING MEDIA NARRATIVE developed shortly after President Obama's inauguration, reflecting negatively on the American people while being completely false. Despite the lack of verifiable evidence, major news agencies and notable bloggers sparked a national discourse by speculating that President Obama was receiving an extraordinary number of threats because of his ethnicity. When a book about the Secret Service was released in 2009, it reported an inside source as saying that threats to the new president had increased about 400 percent. This quickly became a mainstream media joke. This deceptive and erroneous statistic ignores a number of patterns that I observed firsthand while working in the Protective Intelligence Unit at the New York field office and assigned to the PPD.

During my twelve-year employment at the Secret Service, the number of reported threats to our designated protectees grew. This is not in question. However, there is a clear distinction between reported threats and rising overall threat levels. The exponential rise of social media platforms and mobile communication has created an environment in which casual threats can be easily made and reported. Threats, both veiled and direct, made in bars or between friends and relatives were formerly only reported to the Secret Service and investigated when someone who witnessed or heard the threat reported the perpetrator. This changed with the introduction of social media and increased e-mail communication. Threats sent via e-mail may now be easily forwarded, and social media postings containing threats could be shared and "retweeted," allowing any concerned individual reading the threat to launch a Secret Service inquiry. Stories about the "overwhelming" threat level to President Obama overlooked the simple facts that the Secret Service does not publicly publish its threat numbers to the president, and that the overall threat level to President Obama was consistent with past trends.

Agencies are fundamentally territorial, and despite post-9/11 legislative demands to better coordinate investigation operations and intelligence sharing, I've seen little improvement. Protecting an agency's budget and mission will always be the top priority for agency administrators, regardless of congressional mandate. Unless we begin to consolidate the rapidly expanding federal law enforcement staff into a streamlined paradigm, we will continue to see intelligence and investigation failures akin to those linked with the Boston Marathon bombing.

Unfortunately, the trend is shifting in the opposite direction, with about a fifth of federal law enforcement professionals now working for smaller agencies with little investigative jurisdiction, such as the Fish and Wildlife Service and the National Oceanic and Atmospheric Administration. Consider the possibilities if we transferred agents involved in the now-infamous Fish and Wildlife Service raids on the Gibson guitar firm to interrogate suspected terrorists like the Tsarnaev brothers, who were responsible for the Boston bombing.

Chapter 15: GIVING BACK THE GUN AND SHIELD

After nearly five years of service at PPD, it was time to advance in my career. There are no farewells when an officer leaves the PPD. The "ceremony" only requires you to report to the administrative office to hand in your White House pass and key to the White House grounds. Its dullness is the epitome of the term "anticlimactic." As a courtesy, the Executive Office of the President invites you to join the president in the Oval Office for a series of departure photos with your family. I gratefully accepted the opportunity to capture the photograph and felt pleased to be a part of it. Despite our strong political differences, President Obama and his family always treated me with dignity and respect. He was one of the men I would gladly have given my life for. Despite the less than flattering nature of an agent's departure from the PPD, they typically did their best to accommodate departing agents' post-PPD assignment requests, and I was grateful to be assigned to the Baltimore field office, located off Pratt Street in the city's inner harbor area.

I enjoyed criminal investigative casework early in my career, but once you try protection work, there's no going back. Having a front-row seat to the world's most important events is like taking powerful medication. I remembered the moment President George W. Bush spoke from the Oval Office, how I stood just feet behind the camera at the Oval Office door, watching it live, and how, when Bear Stearns collapsed and the gravity of the financial crisis became clear, I was in the limo with President Bush, listening to his take on the situation. I imagined standing in the Oval Office's private reading room while President Bush was sprinting on his exercise bike on the White House patio, looking around at all the mementos he collected as president: a brick from the home of the Taliban's spiritual leader, Mullah Omar; the Glock pistol Saddam Hussein was carrying when he was apprehended; and many more. This was now all part of my personal history, and the recollections were difficult to forget and leave behind.

The case briefly distracted me from the nostalgia I had been feeling since leaving the White House, but it was only for a short time. The case received substantial coverage in the local media, including a front-page story in the Baltimore Sun. I was proud to have helped suffering Marylanders escape the evil of this fraudulent guy. My first live radio appearance was to discuss the matter with WBAL (a radio station that eventually prominently covered my campaign). I was worried about the appearance because the Secret Service had a strong media policy that limited what could be disclosed about a case and our procedures. Despite my reservations, the appearance was wonderful and provided me a taste of what being in the media spotlight was all about.

With the investigation part of the case drawing to an end and the prosecution phase beginning, my task was nearly complete. The fraud case was fulfilling, but it did not satiate my urge to do something more. Seeing the political transformation as we transitioned from one administration to the next from within the White House exacerbated my pain. It appeared to me that the Obama White House personnel lived in a utopian bubble, completely unaware of real-world implications. They discussed policy in utopian terms rather than how to apply legislative solutions in the real world. When a policy not only failed to deliver the expected consequence, but also produced the opposite result, it was ignored.

The Obamacare law is a clear example. Despite the administration's stated goals of increasing health care and cutting costs, the realities have been the exact opposite. As health-care prices continue to grow faster than inflation, and an increasing number of doctors abandon the profession or refuse to take on any more government-sponsored cases, the administration turns a blind eye, seemingly proud of its good intentions but failing to deliver results. The administration persists, despite the angry town hall meetings, dismal results, and abysmal polling, because they are safe within the White House. The president has surrounded himself with supporters who rarely speak truth to power. The people closest to him politically are also those with whom he has personal relationships, and this approach will inevitably lead to a clash between the real world and the artificial world of the presidency.

My primary concern was for my wife and kids, who would have to endure a campaign and potential loss. If I stayed with the Secret Service, my life would be quite steady. All of the journeys to different locations, the coworkers I now considered friends, the exhilaration of a well implemented security strategy, and the stress of the job's expectations were racing through my head. I was fully aware that once I completed the documents indicating my intention to resign my commission as a special agent, I couldn't go back. This was permanent.

The tension of the decision-making process made the short drive from my house in Severna Park to the Baltimore field office seem longer than normal. My wife and I were committed to the strategy, but I kept second-guessing and recalculating. The decision to resign now affected me, Paula, my daughter Isabel, and my unborn daughter Amelia. My mind was in chaos. After all, the life of a special agent is difficult in terms of job requirements, but not in terms of employment stability. I could retire at the age of 49 in just over 12 years with a safe pension, lifetime health insurance coverage, and financial stability.

Chapter 16: FROM BEHIND THE CAMERA TO THE FRONT

Most people, including Secret Service management did not take mY DECISION TO LEAVE the Secret Service and run for the United States Senate seriously. When I awoke that first Monday morning after resigning with no assignment for the first time in nearly two decades, I felt it was best to wait a few weeks before announcing to the public that I was running for Senate.

On Tuesday, May 31, 2011, I was preparing to make the official announcement that I was running for the Maryland Senate seat. That morning, I called one of the Secret Service's deputy assistant directors and left a thorough message, but I did not receive a call back. They knew I was going to run for Senate, but I don't think they realized how serious my plans were. I was determined to change the political atmosphere in what I saw as a winnable contest, and I would not be deterred. No one from the Secret Service ever contacted me to discuss the judgment and its potential consequences for the agency.

My first live interview was set for the afternoon drive-time radio hour with Shari Elliker of WBAL radio. Having appeared on a live radio program once, addressing the fraud case with WBAL, I knew this would be a trial by fire. I paced anxiously and silently, hoping that the appearance would be beneficial and allow me to capitalize on the attention the announcement had received. I found the interview process to be less stressful than I imagined, especially when compared to briefing the White House Situation Room via secure video link from a battle zone in Afghanistan. Despite the fact that thousands of people were listening, I kept reminding myself that it was just me and Shari having a talk, and the impact was evident. Friends and family gave me positive feedback about the radio show. I followed up with appearances on conservative morning radio shows in the Maryland area. Despite my lack of experience with the media, I felt at ease and began to receive emails from listeners who praised my candor and desire to delve into economic concerns. Due to the positive media coverage, donations began to stream into our website, and the foundation of a campaign began to emerge.

The media spotlight intensified throughout the week, and we hit gold just two days after the announcement when Karla, my campaign media liaison, asked me coyly if I would be interested in appearing on Neil Cavuto's show on Fox News Channel. Any opportunity to appear in front of Fox News Channel's vast and dedicated viewership is highly prized among candidates, particularly conservatives. I'd never done live TV before. All of my previous interviews had been on the radio, and I hoped to not only complete the interview but also get it noticed. Arriving at the New York studio and sitting in the green room was an unusual experience. As a Secret Service member for twelve years, I was always surrounded by the media, yet I was never the focus of their attention. I'd been watching Your World with Neil Cavuto for years and walked down the corridor to the studio, convinced that this was the beginning of something extraordinary.

Chapter 17: ISRAEL AND A SURPRISE ENTRANCE INTO THE PRIMARY

During my tenure As a Secret Service agent I worked directly with Israeli security forces, and I've always considered Israel's security to be a personal rather than a political matter. Seeing personally the life-or-death security scenarios encountered by my Israeli counterparts raised my eyes to the serious threat that they confront on a daily basis.

This speaks to an ideology that is uninterested in negotiations or "peace talks"—it is only interested in death, first of Israel and subsequently of the United States. Following President Obama's infamous statement advocating for a return to the 1967 boundaries as the basis for future talks, I decided that rather than simply speaking about Israel, I wanted to act and show my support. Using my own money, I decided to attend a pro-Israel protest planned by radio presenter Glenn Beck in the summer of 2011. I had no idea at the time how the trip would affect the path of my campaign and my life.

Following the rally, I was planning to attend a dinner with Israeli and US officials, and some more guests. There was some miscommunication over seating allocations, and I was accidentally seated next to Senator Mike Lee of Utah. In our ensuing talk, I discovered Senator Lee to be a real, impassioned champion of his ideas over politics—a rare occurrence among public leaders. I informed him that I was running for the US Senate in Maryland, and we had a nearly two-hour conversation about political philosophy, economics, and constitutional law. Our conversation was invigorating, and I found it comforting to know that there were still some "good guys" around. I was grateful to be able to meet with Senator Lee again after returning home, and I was overjoyed when he agreed to endorse me. Senator Lee's backing humbled and honored me, as I had little name recognition or money and was running in a campaign that was unlikely to win under the best of conditions. This started a relationship that helped my campaign gain a credible, national profile among elected officials, which is more difficult to achieve than a credible media profile.

Regardless of the fortunate circumstances that led to my meeting with Senator Lee, starting a Republican campaign organization in a blue state from scratch was a daunting endeavor that necessitated a meticulous approach. The campaign schedule filled up rapidly, and I spent hours each day driving from event to event. Maryland is an awkward state that is too small to fly, so we spent all of our campaign travels on the road. Given my experience as an agent throughout three presidential campaigns, I thought I had a solid grasp of the workload and the constant stress. But when it comes to your own campaign, things are completely different. There are no days off on a campaign, and on the busiest days, I would give up to ten speeches. Eating became a luxury, and I was able to locate bathrooms in every area of Maryland. I spent most of my time in the car between campaign stops, trying to raise money over the phone.

I declared my candidacy in May 2011, and for months, I had the political spotlight to myself. As potential Republican nominees dropped out of the campaign, the path to the Republican primary nomination became apparent. But just as the campaign appeared to be gaining traction, I received an email from a friend with a statement of candidacy for the 2012 Republican nomination from former deputy assistant secretary of defense Richard Douglas. His resume was remarkable, and my wife and I recognized instantly that the political environment had shifted. The nomination campaign would be considerably harder today, but I was more motivated than ever. I didn't quit the Secret Service to lose the Republican primary, and while I welcomed competitors, I wasn't going to lose to them.

Chapter 18: THE CAMPAIGN HEATS UP

At the Maryland Republican Convention that October, my campaign had a large hospitality section. It was an excellent opportunity to build further buzz for the campaign. However, some of the attention we received did not match our expectations. After a fantastic night of connecting with supporters, I received a phone call from Brandon, a campaign staffer, who informed me that his tires were flat. The next morning, I received another phone call from my campaign manager informing me that his tires were also flat. Someone pounded nails into the tires of Brandon, Jim, and a third campaign staffer. One week earlier, we discovered nails in my pregnant wife's tires, indicating that someone was sending us a dangerous message. Sometimes the best retaliation for such nasty tactics is to utilize them to expose your opponent. We published a news release detailing the occurrences and publicly humiliated the individuals who perpetrated them. We've never found nails in our tires again.

The team's primary day on April 3 was exhilarating. There was little accurate polling on the Republican primary battle, so all we could do was hope for the best. Knowing how much work we put into the race, I was cautiously optimistic that we could win. The night was an emotional rollercoaster. As the county-by-county results came in, we would have a comfortable lead, only to see Rich close in, only for us to move ahead with another county victory. Around 10:00 p.m. that night, the results began to flip in our favor, and as our lead grew, so did my excitement. Rich finally gave up at 11:00 p.m. because the math was too difficult for him.

It was a moment of sheer happiness. Given where I began, I never imagined I would get to this stage. The enthusiastic, ecstatic expressions on the faces of the hundreds of fans and family members who had assembled to celebrate were a better prize than any political success.

It reached a climax when a Baltimore-area radio presenter named Sean Casey emailed me asking for a remark. After receiving demands from every major network, cable channel, print, and internet publication, I felt compelled to react to Sean. He was fair and respectful to me throughout the early stages of my campaign, when few people gave me a chance. I agreed to do his show that week, knowing that once my voice reached the airways, the door to more media would be wide open. I notified Karla to start taking interview requests, and the rush began. Although I made no attempt to conceal the fact that I had personal contacts with several of the agents engaged in the incident, I felt strongly that I should not be held responsible for publishing their names, given the delicate nature of the situation for the agents' families. My brother's name was meant to be kept out of the media, along with the other agents involved, but someone with access to the Secret Service records of the incident released it to the Huffington Post.

With my sister-in-law on my mind, I called my brother again, and he answered. I told him I was furious and started yelling at him, upset about the devastation this was causing our family. He explained that he had no understanding what was going on and that after breakfast, he was told to board a bus and depart Colombia. My brother revealed that one of his team members had returned to the hotel with a woman, and he overheard her complaining loudly in the corridor late at night. He and a Colombian police officer stationed on that floor of the hotel tried to aid her. He repeatedly told me that he didn't understand what was going on since he didn't speak Spanish and she didn't speak English. He said he had no dealings with prostitutes.

I was honest and upfront in my public comments regarding the issue and how it was handled, and that is now history. Personally, I was outraged by the White House's patronizing approach to the scandal and its aftermath. These men made terrible mistakes, and almost all of them paid the price by losing their careers, spouses, and reputations.

The Secret Service acted fast and fired those who breached the rules and embarrassed the agency, but in the end, they were all guys who would have sacrificed their lives for the president of the United States and his family without hesitation. Although their missteps have become the topic of a major international scandal, their actions have never jeopardized operational security, and I believe the president's harsh remarks were unwarranted. He failed to recognize that this was a prevalent pattern of behavior among his own White House personnel and other federal divisions.

Despite the realities of both staff and agent behavior on the ground, the administration publicly chastised the Secret Service while making no mention of cleaning up its own home. The regulations appeared to apply only when there was a political advantage to be had. Publicly criticizing the Secret Service was a low-risk political move for the administration. The White House spin team recognized that the Secret Service would not defend this heinous act, allowing the president to seem as the disciplinarian. I blame the president's staff for utilizing the situation to boost their image, although it is widely known that some of his own personnel have failed to maintain the public call for greater standards of conduct.

Chapter 19: A POLITICAL LOSS, AND WHY ACTION MATTERS

By the early summer of 2012, the Colombia issue had subsided enough for me to concentrate solely on the rest of my campaign. We worked tirelessly throughout the summer, knocking on countless doors, making thousands of phone calls, shaking tens of thousands of hands, and attending every crab feast, barbecue, community function, and parade that fit into our calendar. Despite the tremendous efforts of my staff, volunteers, and family, I was not optimistic on Election Day 2012. I had no cause to be. An unexpected and terrible turn of circumstances occurred late in the campaign, making victory the longest of long shots. The campaign staff and I were absolutely surprised in late September when Rob Sobhani, a twice-failed Republican nomination candidate, decided to run as an independent with less than a month until the election. And he had a $6 million war chest to fund his operations in the final weeks of the campaign.

Although the campaign was realistic about our weak possibilities at this time, we refused to give up and continued the fight on our own field. We received the most grassroots support and quadrupled our phone calls and door knocking efforts. At this moment, our best hope was to finish in second place. I believed that if we could at least hold on to the Republican base on Election Day, it would demonstrate the force of sheer determination. Our media budget was dwarfed by the competition, and I had no political experience to speak of. Yet we were still able to communicate a clear set of ideas and principles amid the electoral fog of both the presidential election and the negative advertising produced by the other candidates in my campaign. Election night would be emotionally challenging for me, Paula, Isabel, and the staff. While traveling to the hotel ballroom near BWI Airport, which we shared with Congressman Andy Harris, it became clear that everything was over. We were going to lose, and no amount of emotion or desire to change the country's path could make up for it.

Unfortunately, there are no Silver Medals in politics. Only one candidate is sworn in as a United States senator, and only one hand is laid on the Bible in our Capitol, and it will not be mine. My daughter Isabel was devastated. Throughout the campaign, I was unable to convince her that our chances of winning were slim. She believed in her father, and no one, even me, was going to convince her differently. I took her up, held her tightly, and shed a tear as she again asked me why we lost. It was difficult to regain my calm, but I knew I had work to accomplish that evening. I had to contact Senator Cardin and congratulate him on his victory, followed by a concession statement in front of the hotel ballroom's many supporters, staff, and media representatives.

My conversation with the recently reelected Senator Cardin was neither awkward nor bitter. We agreed on very little politically, but never engaged in personal attacks and had become friendly while campaigning. He complimented me for running a dignified campaign, said he recognized the amount of effort I put in, and wished me luck in the future, to which I answered in kind. After hanging up the phone, I prepared to give my final statement as Maryland's Republican Senate candidate in 2012. When you observe the difference between our lives here in the United States and the lives of people in practically every other country on the planet, your desire to defend the ideals that have made us unique will only grow. We are living in a political moment in which fundamental American ideas—the rule of law, limited government, and individual liberty—have come under severe attack, despite our country's unquestionable riches, power, and success, which make it a beacon and example for the rest of the world. If you feel that today is not the best it will ever be, and that tomorrow may and will be better, you must be willing to fight for it. Fighting for it demands action, not words. Complaining about the country's political trajectory may temporarily ease some of the frustration associated with an unwelcome national decline, but it will not turn the tide.

Several developments in recent months have caused me concern. The events themselves have resulted in the deaths of innocent individuals and public servants, which is disturbing enough, but the media and administration's handling of the situation has exacerbated the repercussions. Honest media coverage of these instances would have rapidly dispelled any suspicions or rumors of a cover-up, and ironically, the media's concealment of the stories only added to the scandal narrative. Some of these concerns, such as the Fast and Furious affair and the Benghazi tragedy, involve the types of complicated security and military operations that I have witnessed throughout my career, and the errors are obvious. I can only imagine what goes on behind the scenes, on secure conference lines and in situation rooms, when administration personnel are engrossed in weaving their stories. The Boston Marathon terror attack is another example of a security failure that killed innocents. At least in the instance of Boston, the government came forward and classified the bombing as "terror" in the president's second remark on the incident. There were obvious security flaws that allowed these terrorists to move freely throughout the country and travel back and forth to Russia without triggering any red lights.

Most people believe they know the truth regarding these significant topics in our country's contemporary history, but I know there is much that goes unreported, and mainstream media coverage of these subjects has been inadequate at best. In the following chapters, we will focus on three particularly tragic examples that demonstrate how the growing size of government bureaucracy has created an environment of detachment, where no one is truly responsible, where there is always another layer in an organization to blame for wrongdoing—and where innocent people have died as a result.

Chapter 20: THE REAL SCANDAL OF "FAST AND FURIOUS"

The heroic and tragic death of Border Patrol Officer Brian Terry in December 2010 ignited the powder keg of a national controversy that is still burning. The operation, dubbed "Fast and Furious" due to some of the investigative targets' proclivity for street racing, has been the subject of congressional inquiries, media investigations, internal US government investigations, and public scrutiny, but the true story of what occurred remains unknown.

There are several reasons the truth has not come to light. The issue of weapons trafficking, unlike trafficking in narcotics or counterfeit documents (which I routinely investigated as a Secret Service agent), includes a web of political interests that even the most expert political operative would struggle to unravel. Despite the ongoing obscurity around the case, some facts are evident. I will outline what is known, but the burning question remains: were Fast and Furious weapons deployed on US territory, and why did the Department of Justice fail to take preventative measures?

The operation began in 2009 as an ATF investigation to prevent the flow of guns purchased illegally in the United States and transported across the Mexican border. I've worked on cases alongside ATF officers, and I can certainly say that they're an elite bunch of men and women dedicated to service and nation. They are up against Mexican drug cartel members who employ "straw buyers" to obtain guns, according to law officials. A straw buyer is someone who buys a firearm on behalf of someone who, for a number of reasons, is not eligible to do so themselves.

Border Patrol Agent Brian Terry and his four-member BORTAC (Border Patrol Tactical) squad came under heavy, surprise fire after detaining five illegal border crossers, turning the case tragic and into a national news story. Agent Terry was mortally injured in the brief but intense exchange of gunfire. One of the suspects, Manuel Osorio Arellanes, was apprehended, wounded but still alive. Weapons used by the criminals were found near the body of the critically injured Agent Terry, and they were traced back to the Lone Wolf Trading Company in Glendale, Arizona. From there, the national scandal began to unravel.

Internal and external politics, election cycles, disagreements between the Department of Justice and the ATF, Second Amendment rights, and petty internal office squabbles all contributed to the Fast and Furious debacle. To understand why I place a large portion of the blame on the Department of Justice and why I believe Brian Terry's death will not be the last, I must first distinguish between initiating, investigating, and prosecuting crimes at the federal, state, and local levels. This essential distinction is critical to the Fast and Furious case.

When I was a young police officer with the New York City Police Department, it was not uncommon to see a street crime while on duty, arrest the culprit, and then provide a written affidavit to establish probable cause. Probable cause is required for any arrest, regardless of jurisdiction. At the NYPD, we witnessed a crime, apprehended the culprit, and then acquired investigative information.

Establishing probable cause and making an arrest in the federal system typically work in the other direction. Federal agents normally conduct a comprehensive investigation of the case first, establishing probable cause in the process, before calling an "intake" assistant United States attorney (AUSA) to see if he will accept the case for future prosecution. If the AUSA decides to prosecute the matter in federal court, arrest warrants will be issued and the suspects will be taken into jail, but only after a large amount of evidence has been gathered. Few AUSAs prefer to handle cases that could go to trial, therefore the bar for acceptance by the attorney is high. Typically, the AUSA wants enough evidence to induce a plea deal, so a trial is not even a possibility. Numbers are important in federal justice politics because they can help politicians and officials advance their careers. Successful federal prosecutions, and falling crime rates, are electoral gold. This gives US lawyers a strong incentive to avoid taking on cases in which they have even a slight probability of losing.

Why does the process matter? Because a "PC arrest" (short for probable cause arrest) is an uncommon and strongly discouraged federal law enforcement tool. Every day, state and local police officers employ probable cause arrest authority to keep our communities safe. However, federal agents, many of whom are former police officers, are highly advised against making this type of arrest. They must follow the established federal protocol of conducting an investigation and obtaining AUSA approval before making an arrest. It may appear illogical that well-trained, well-educated federal agents cannot perform what our police officers do on a daily basis, but that is exactly the case. A probable cause arrest is inherently unpredictable, and unpredictability is the enemy of our federal judicial system. Everyone, including the magistrate judges, the intake AUSA, the assigned AUSA, and the US Marshals Service, which will oversee the prisoner, has reasonably constant work schedules. The quickest way to get on the wrong side of the US Attorney's Office is to begin making PC arrests late at night before exhausting all investigation channels, completing mountains of paperwork, and scheduling an arrest with the AUSA. Yes, an appointment.

Unless there is a legitimate urgency, a PC arrest is a near career death sentence. If you get into trouble with an AUSA, none of your future cases are likely to be prosecuted. In this arrangement, the AUSA wields considerable influence, as evidenced by the PC arrest scenario. Based on my expertise, I believe this power structure played a critical part in the catastrophic Fast and Furious operation.

The widely held perception surrounding the operation, which has been reinforced by the media, is that ATF officers allowed guns to "walk," i.e., be purchased illegally and untracked, resulting in Brian Terry's untimely death. After reading and examining many reports of the events surrounding the probe, I do not believe this is the case. According to all reports, the seven ATF officers in Group VII, commanded by case agent Hope MacAllister, were devoted, non ideological federal operators who really wanted to stop illegal guns running into Mexico. Allowing weapons to "walk" is not a sanctioned investigative strategy, and I doubt Group VII intended this.

Trafficking firearms from straw buyers is a federal crime, but if no one is prepared to prosecute the case, it's like a tree falling in the woods— no one hears it. According to Katherine Eban of Forbes magazine's article from June 27, 2012, "By January 2010, the agents had identified 20 individuals who had paid almost $350,000 in cash for more than 650 firearms. According to Rep. Issa's congressional committee, Group VII had enough evidence to make arrests and close the matter immediately."

In my experience researching comparable federal cases involving the purchase of contraband, Assistant United States Attorney Emory Hurley, along with MacAllister and Group VII operatives, might have easily pursued prosecution. The evidence was overwhelming. It featured frequent cash purchases of expensive firearms by buyers who lacked the financial resources to support this type of activity. In the summer of 2010, a straw buyer working with Group VII agent John Dodson delivered guns to a suspected gun trafficker and produced wiretap recordings of the illegal transactions, but no arrests were made. In response to questions about the investigation's progress, former ATF attaché in Mexico Darren Gil commented, "Again, spring time it got to the point of … at what point are we going to close this investigation?" I mean, after 500 or so seizures, I believe you should have gathered enough data to demonstrate or prove your point. It was not only my stance, but also that of Chief [Dan Kumor]. He answers, "Yes, you're correct." And he says, 'So when are they going to close this down?' And we both agreed that this thing ought to be shut down."

Never in my experience as a federal agent have I heard of an investigation with this much evidence yet no indictments or arrest warrants. Receiving judicial clearance for a federal wiretap requires a tremendous quantity of evidence. Before a federal judge approves a wiretap, every practical tool in the investigator's arsenal must be exhausted. The fact that Group VII obtained wiretap power suggests to me that the case had progressed much beyond the point of justifiable suspicion and was known to DOJ headquarters. Any attempt by DOJ headquarters to claim ignorance of the circumstances before Agent Terry's unfortunate death is suspect at best. The federal wiretap application was signed in the spring of 2010 on behalf of Assistant Attorney General Lanny Breuer by the Department of Justice's Office of Enforcement Operations.

In an ideal world, Group VII agents would have stopped the flow of weapons crossing the border and conducted probable cause arrests, just like any local police officer. However, it is not a perfect world, and in federal law enforcement, an ever-growing army of agents insulated within competing agencies and rarely interacting with one another are forced to compete for the limited time of the US Attorney's Office, and you cannot afford to be on the receiving end of their wrath or you will be ignored. Combine this dynamic with the bureaucratic DOJ and its ever-expanding layers of structure meant to shield those at the top from having to accept responsibility for what is actually happening on their watch, and you have the recipe for disaster.

The fact that an arrest was made within twenty-four hours of Border Patrol Agent Brian Terry's death confirms my beliefs that probable cause was available and arrests should have occurred. Jaime Avila, suspected of acquiring two of the weapons discovered alongside Agent Terry's body, was arrested, and nineteen more people were indicted two weeks later, on January 19, 2011. Is this making sense to you? Seven veteran ATF agents investigate a gun trafficking organization for nearly a year, utilizing every instrument known to modern law enforcement, and they are unable to build a legally viable case. However, within twenty-four hours of Agent Terry's death, the DOJ and the Arizona US Attorney's Office determine that the case is worth prosecuting. This smacks of prosecutorial laziness, incompetence, and hubris. I am convinced that the US Attorney's Office was concerned about losing the case if it went to trial, despite the plenty of evidence, and opted to let it fester. The insensitive DOJ bureaucracy and diffused responsibilities encouraged US attorneys to achieve high prosecution numbers that could be sold politically rather than pursue cases that were more valuable to the public. They were only motivated to action when they recognized there would be serious political implications from Agent Terry's highly publicized death and the subsequent investigation. Their carelessness and lack of integrity had real-world implications, and despite many warnings from ATF officers on the ground, the DOJ only intervened when it came at a political cost.

The US Attorney's Office ordered Group VII ATF agents to accept a losing proposition. They were unable to arrest the suspects, despite having more than enough evidence, because the AUSA frowned on probable cause arrests. However, they could not quit the case and let the arms trade continue uninterrupted. Regardless of the ATF's actions, weapons were going to "walk" across the border, and prosecutorial and bureaucratic incompetence would be to blame. No federal agent wants to be in a situation where carnage is the outcome of a crime they could have averted.

Furthermore, Department of Justice headquarters cannot claim ignorance of the possible dangers of delay, as AUSA Joe Cooley was personally briefed on the case's significance on March 5, 2010. Cooley attended the meeting at ATF headquarters on behalf of Assistant Attorney General Lanny Breuer, and Group VII supervisor David Voth briefed him on the case's alarming specifics. According to ATF officers, the presence of a DOJ headquarters person at these briefings was unprecedented. Furthermore, according to the Joint Staff Report prepared for Congress, Robert Champion, the special agent in charge of the ATF's Dallas office, voiced concern about the increasing number of firearms sourced to Fast and Furious. During a video conference, he inquired, "What are we doing about this?"

The DOJ headquarters, represented at the conference by AUSA Cooley, responded that the magnitude of unlawful trafficking was "an acceptable practice." It wasn't. When it was discovered that Fast and Furious firearms were used in the murders of Mexican civilians, the media went into a frenzy. However, few journalists thought to inquire whether Fast and Furious guns were used on US soil. It still baffles me that this question has escaped numerous investigative journalists. With nearly a hundred high-powered weapons seized from crime sites in Mexico, my data study suggests that this is only the tip of the iceberg.

Looking at these facts, it is not difficult to assume that these weapons were not only discovered but also utilized on American soil, despite the lack of media attention on the subject. Federal limitations prevent trace-data specifics, such as the federal firearm licensee who sold the firearm, from being made public, but I'm afraid the connection will be discovered eventually. One of these guns will be linked to a crime on US soil. It's only a question of time. This hazardous result of the Department of Justice's failure to forcefully and immediately combat the illegal trafficking of high-powered rifles has astounded some, but it does not surprise me.

Chapter 21: BENGHAZI: WHO GAVE THE ORDER TO STAND DOWN?

During my twelve-year career as a special agent with the United States Secret Service, I was fortunate to work with some of the world's top military and law enforcement personnel. I was continuously awed by the integrity of the men and women in our military who, for little pay and even less renown, agree to risk their lives to safeguard this country so that millions of Americans can sleep soundly. The battle-hardened special operators who served as a counterassault team in Indonesia and were willing to do whatever it took to keep the president safe, as well as the Delta Force operator in Afghanistan whose blank stare clearly captured the emotional suppression of everything he had seen and done in service to our country, were inspiring portraits of courage and sacrifice to me.

Although being a Secret Service agent is a hard job, I never felt underappreciated or underpaid. I always regretted that my words of gratitude to the soldiers of our military whose paths I crossed never quite expressed the depth of my appreciation. These men and women work long hours in the roughest temperatures and most dangerous areas in the world, all for very little money. My brief and occasionally imperfect words of appreciation were a small tribute of gratitude to a group of men and women who deserved considerably more.

When I first heard about the horrific events in Benghazi, Libya, on September 11, 2012, I thought it was a mistake or bad reporting. I had extensive experience serving with the Diplomatic Security Service, the US Department of State's security and protection branch, having been assigned to numerous protective tasks for foreign leaders, dignitaries, and, of course, the president. I couldn't believe the claims that Christopher Stevens, the ambassador to Libya, was missing. I couldn't picture an ambassador going missing and potentially dying under their watch.

Given that they were performing operations in an active conflict zone, the Diplomatic Security Service was undoubtedly accompanied by a fully equipped and staffed security unit. I was particularly disturbed by tales of a communication breakdown during the attack on our diplomatic mission in Benghazi. During my years in the White House, continuously trailing the president, I witnessed how he and his senior officials had rapid access to information. When anything noteworthy occurs, the president or a relevant cabinet member is notified via several channels of communication. They receive email, phone briefings, personal briefings, and a seemingly limitless supply of briefing documents that are regularly updated. The purported lack of information reaching the president and secretary of state about the mounting disaster in Libya contradicted my firsthand experience within the eighteen-acre White House compound.

Analyzing Benghazi as someone who has seen the inner workings of the White House and made a career of risk management and mitigation, there are three specific areas of concern that I found particularly alarming, and they all relate to the DC web of bureaucracy impeding operations on the ground. First, the inadequacy of the security detail was completely out of proportion to the threat level in an active conflict zone. Second, the information stream disseminated by the White House and other administration surrogates was inconsistent with any previous crisis-management message strategy I had seen in two presidential administrations, and it directly contradicted the accounts of personnel on the ground, and information from within the government. Third, the survivors of the Benghazi attack appear to have vanished, and neither the media nor our elected representatives were given access to interview them.

My first concern is about the appointed protection team and the security plan in place on the night of the attack. When a US government figure is assigned a security detail by one of the rising army of siloed and unique federal entities that provide this service, manpower and equipment are allotted based on an intelligence-based threat assessment. This evaluation is a thorough examination of the present and possible dangers that may threaten the protectee and any supporting personnel. It takes into account the protector's diplomatic status, the geographic region in which he operates, and his potential worth to our adversaries as an assault target. Using this methodology, the agents who design the protection plan can determine the number of agents to assign to the protective detail; the weapons they carry; the number of vehicles required and the armor capabilities of those vehicles; the number, if any, of special weapons teams to assign; the use of military assets, including special operations forces if necessary; the level of security required at the physical sites where the protectee will live, work, and visit; and

I frequently worked with the Diplomatic Security Service's excellent agents and was startled to discover from a source that Ambassador Stevens did not have a Mobile Security Deployment (MSD) tactical unit assigned to him during his time in Benghazi on September 11, 2012. This cadre of highly trained special weapons operators typically works on high-risk protection assignments, carrying advanced weapons meant to deter and counter any prospective attack on a high-value target. Why weren't these men, the DSS's best-trained and most talented protection agents, deployed when a US ambassador was present in an active combat zone? Less than a year ago, former ambassador Gene Cretz and up to twenty-one members of this expert force were in Libya. Why were they removed?

It is apparent that DSS personnel realized the security footprint assigned to Ambassador Stevens was insufficient, and despite their warnings and requests, the inadequate protection plan was tragically maintained. Ambassador Stevens was aware of the inadequate security and expressed concern about the loss of the MSD teams in a May 2012 e-mail to State Department official John Moretti, stating that he and his team "would feel much safer if we could keep two MSD teams with us through this period." The request was denied.

Eric Nordstrom, the DSS regional security officer in charge of the detail assigned to Ambassador Stevens, testified to senators following the Benghazi incident that he asked five DSS agents to be stationed at the mission. Deputy Assistant Secretary Charlene Lamb responded by saying, "[she] believed the Benghazi post did not need any Diplomatic Security special agents because there was a residential safe haven to fall back on in an emergency, but that she thought the best course of action was to assign three agents."

Three DSS agents in an active war zone, with no MSD tactical assistance, and directed by a bureaucrat with little security background is a startling display of either incompetence or wrongdoing. Unfortunately, that is entirely consistent with what I have seen from isolated career bureaucrats who overvalued their own abilities at the expense of qualified specialists' analyses.

What makes Lamb's denial of the security request even more perplexing is that, in my experience, the request for even five DSS agents (the actual number present on the night of the attack due to temporarily assigned duty personnel being in country) was grossly insufficient and was most likely motivated by frustration with the bureaucratic process. It suggests that the DSS and/or the ambassador were willing to tolerate an elevated security risk because they believed it wasn't worth fighting the State Department for appropriate resources.

Mr. Nordstrom further testified before the House Oversight and Government Reform Committee that Lamb "wanted to keep the number of US security personnel in Benghazi artificially low." He also told the regional director of the agency's Bureau of Near Eastern Affairs, "For me, the Taliban is on the inside of the building."

Nordstrom's words are concerning since they refer to political decisions rather than those based on proven protection procedures and experience-driven danger evaluations from a security professional. I understand his angst.

The insufficient security footprint was not overlooked by military leaders in the region looking to help. Lieutenant Colonel Andrew Wood noticed the disparity between the security proposed by State Department bureaucrats and what was actually required after a number of foreign governments and non-governmental organizations (NGOs) withdrew from the area. According to a committee report, he stated, "It was clear to me that we were the last flag flying in Benghazi." We were the last thing on their list of targets to eliminate from Benghazi.

To put it in perspective, when I prepared President Obama's security operation in Afghanistan, thousands of individuals from federal law enforcement and the US military were involved. This operation was held on a guarded US military base, and despite the tremendous level of cooperation from everyone listed, I had severe security concerns.

Now compare this to the protective perimeter around Ambassador Stevens on the night of the attack. He had just five DSS agents, no Mobile Security Deployment tactical squad, and no assigned military special forces assistance. Does this seem sensible to you? It does not require significant US Secret Service training to determine that the officials who inserted themselves into the security decision-making chain were driven by politics rather than a genuine concern for security. They were more concerned with spreading the president's narrative that "al-Qaeda is on the run" than protecting our diplomats and military who defend this country. If Ambassador Stevens, Sean Smith, Glen Doherty, and Ty Woods had realized earlier that their lives were the result of a series of terrible wagers made by bureaucrats to secure their political careers, they could still be alive today.

Of course, politics getting in the way of security is not new. I was involved in a number of security operations where senior White House and other department officials sought to alter the security strategy for political purposes, but I never let it affect our operation. I was always confident that PPD leadership would defend my decisions. Anytime there was a disagreement between staff and the Secret Service, we had to "kick it up the chain" to a senior member of the agency who would back us up. When a conflict escalated to PPD management, security usually won out over politics. So, why was Eric Nordstrom ignored?

I assume it was for political reasons, both within the State Department and in greater electoral politics. The president's reelection campaign was in full gear at the time of the incident, and political successes trumped almost everything for a staff member. If Lamb and others in the State Department admitted, less than two months before the election, that the situation in Libya had deteriorated dramatically, there would be serious consequences. It would be proof that the president's hallmark foreign policy objectives in the Middle East were about to fail. It would demonstrate that terrorists remained a very genuine threat to Americans, which would not earn President Obama more votes. Any staff member who participated in the decision to openly admit a deteriorating security situation would risk losing a future promotion or a coveted new assignment.

However, Lamb and her cadre of State Department officials neglected to consider that by assigning DSS protection to Ambassador Stevens, they would be forced to deal with agents and supervisors who refused to play politics. Nordstrom's nonpolitical stance allowed him to honestly assess the situation and request support appropriate to the threat level. The issue became confused only when persons with political rather than security objectives were involved in the decision-making process. Lamb and others most likely assumed that nothing would happen to our personnel in Benghazi, and when offered military resources at no cost to the State Department, her staff responded that Lamb was hesitant to accept this support because it would be "embarrassing to continue to have to rely on DOD [Department of

Defense] assets to protect our mission."

Her obvious concern for political embarrassment rather than the safety of American servicemen reflects the widespread belief among our bureaucratic elite that they can hide among the diffuse responsibility of their massive organizations. After all, with a bureaucracy as huge and infamous as the State Department's, there must be an underling to blame or a memo they can claim they missed in the unlikely occasion that something catastrophic occurs. Secretary of State Hillary Clinton, an outspoken supporter of expansive government, failed to recognize the hypocrisy of her own ideology when she testified before the House Foreign Affairs Committee that cables addressed specifically to her requesting an increased security footprint in Benghazi did not actually reach her. Clinton stated, "They [the cables] don't all come to me. They are reported via the bureaucracy."

What saddens me the most is that the bureaucratic elite probably sees this tragedy as "the price of doing business," and that the security teams, despite their enthusiasm to serve in Benghazi, were simply following orders, despite what I consider a criminally insufficient protection plan.

Not only was the security decision-making process politicized prior to the attack, but decisions made during the attack were also seriously inadequate and did not adhere to what I recall as standard protocol for such a major incident.

Following the 1979 Iranian hostage crisis and subsequent studies on how to avoid similar events from happening again, the military developed a global response plan for attacks on American embassies abroad. As a result, we had military forces ready and willing to undertake a rescue attempt for our personnel during the Benghazi attack, but a number of still unknown reasons stopped them from obtaining orders to deploy until nearly five hours after the initial assault began. Nothing happened when a military unit was sent from a training mission in Croatia to Southern Europe and activated to support the Benghazi operation. This is where their narrative concludes.

We must ask: who issued the order to stand down, and why?

The failure of FEST, a multi agency team, to act is even more concerning. FEST stands for Foreign Emergency Support Team, and it is made up of highly trained professionals from a variety of federal departments that are especially entrusted with providing quick assistance to US personnel in crisis overseas. The fact that this team was not activated is beyond suspicious, given that their duty is to respond to situations similar to those that transpired in Benghazi. It's like ordering the Secret Service to stand down during an attack on the president.

Another noteworthy example of how the Benghazi attack was mishandled is the plainly deceptive information stream that came from the administration following the attack. Based on my experience working in two presidential administrations, there are safeguards in place to ensure that only designated personnel in charge of the administration's communications share information after rigorous vetting. I've never been engaged with a presidential visit, home or foreign, where message control wasn't a top focus. However, the president and the State Department's response to the Benghazi incident was blatantly false and politically motivated.

The fact that the Benghazi incident occurred so close to the presidential election certainly sparked a rush of activity and worry in and around the White House. When the White House is conducting routine governmental business, it hums with activity. When that hum is disrupted, everything changes. Staffers begin to walk hurriedly, facial expressions of fear become apparent, motorcades begin to line up on West Executive Avenue, and high-ranking government officials who are rarely seen in the White House begin to appear in the crowded hallways of the West Wing.

When the attack happened at 9:40 p.m. It was 3:40 p.m. at the White House, according to local time in Benghazi. This is the pinnacle of the presidential workday. It is highly doubtful that the first item of information the president heard was about a gathering of demonstrators outraged by the now-infamous Internet video mocking Muhammad. This is significant because, while we now know that the protest story is false, if there is no evidence that a protest was ever mentioned by any of the personnel on the ground who were actively communicating with Washington, one must question why the administration completely fabricated such a story. Lying about what happened that night is a dishonor to the guys who died in the attack. I observed crisis management in action at the White House. Each administration has its own set of goals and a strategy for dealing with breaking news. Clearly, the administration's top priority was political spin, followed by safety and security. The facts revealed by the State Department's Accountability Review Board show that there was a purposeful attempt to conceal the reality of what happened at the diplomatic station in Benghazi on September 11, 2012.

The ARB report reveals how, within minutes of the incident, an agent from the Diplomatic Security Service (known as ARSO 1), while fleeing and safeguarding Ambassador Stevens, handed him his cell phone. Stevens then began calling for aid. According to the report, Stevens sought aid from "local contacts" and the Tripoli embassy. Also, the report mentions a 9:50 p.m. Stevens and the deputy chief of mission, Gregory Hicks, spoke about the attack during a local time conversation. According to Hicks' story, which he shared with Utah Representative Jason Chaffetz during congressional hearings, Ambassador Stevens exclaimed to Hicks over the phone, "We're under attack. Hicks also told how he "immediately called into Washington to trigger all the mechanisms."

The embassy in Tripoli was notified of the attack about 9:45 p.m. local time, established a command center, and contacted Washington. Following the embassy's notice of the incident, Department of Defense officers moved an unarmed surveillance drone, which arrived at 11:10 p.m. Local time: "shortly before the DS [Diplomatic Security] team departed."

According to the report, the communication with Tripoli did not indicate a protest, but rather an attack. Furthermore, in a "Ops Alert" issued shortly after the attack began, the State Department Operations Center notified senior department officials, the White House Situation Room, and others that the Benghazi compound was under attack and that "approximately twenty armed people fired shots; explosions have been heard as well." Two hours later, the Operations Center issued an alert that al-Qaeda-linked Ansar al-Sharia (AAS) claimed responsibility for the attack and had called Neither notice noting that there had been a protest near the scene of the attacks.

Several hours later, the report states, "In Washington, at 10:32 p.m., an officer in the National Military Command Center at the Pentagon, after receiving initial reports of the incident from the State Department, notified the Office of the Secretary of Defense and the Joint Staff." The intelligence was swiftly communicated to Secretary of Defense Leon E. Panetta and Chairman of the Joint Chiefs of Staff General Martin E. Dempsey. Secretary Panetta and General Dempsey arrived at the White House for a previously scheduled meeting with the president at 11:00 p.m., some 80 minutes after the attack began. The Defense Department said principals addressed various responses to the ongoing issue.

Our role in the Libyan crisis in the months leading up to the Benghazi attack left a significant intelligence, military, and DSS presence in the region and on the ground, particularly following the demise of Libyan tyrant Muammar Gaddafi. It is exceedingly unlikely that all of these trained and motivated professionals provided incorrect information to their Washington, DC, chain of command. Furthermore, with the pervasive existence of smartphones, Internet-based radio transmissions, satellite phones, e-mail, confidential computer networks, and airborne surveillance technologies, a full communication breakdown with senior authorities in Washington is virtually unthinkable. According to accounts on the incident, contact was immediate and ongoing, with status updates coming from both the ground in Benghazi and the embassy in Tripoli—none of which mentioned any protest. It's ludicrous to think that the government and its allies believed the Benghazi attack was the result of a demonstration over an anti-Muslim Internet video.

Despite all this information, the government shifted into damage-control mode. Just one day after the incident, the White House issued a statement saying, "Since our founding, the United States has been a nation that respects all faiths." We oppose any attempts to disparage others' religious beliefs.

Notice the administration's careful use of words in its attempt to create a theme around the attack. The choice of wording purposely deflects blame away from the president's foreign policy decisions and instead emphasizes on religious persecution. They were also cautious not to state that the offending video was the cause of the attack, but they were clearly establishing the basis for a theme by merely linking the attack to religion, although they had no evidence that the video and the attack were related. They were testing the message without committing to it, which is a frequent strategy in political circles. "Trial balloon" messaging is a regular process in which a message is released and the team attentively monitors how the public and media react.

Initially, when it appeared that the press was buying into the Internet video explanation, the White House hallways were probably bustling with excitement. More frustrating is the fact that their hubris over the lies they were spouting prompted them to spend taxpayer money to support the administration's narrative. Our government paid $70,000 on an advertising campaign in Pakistan immediately following the attack to separate the US from the Internet video, which they knew had nothing to do with the events in Benghazi.

As the days of early September passed, the administration pushed its message forward. On September 14, Secretary of State Hillary Clinton declared, "We've seen the heavy assault on our post in Benghazi that claimed the lives of those heroic guys. We've seen hatred and violence aimed against American embassies over a horrific Internet video that we had nothing to do with." The video's reference to the attack reinforces the message. The administration once again waited for serious media investigations to begin. This did not happen.

The administration's false explanation of the origin of the Benghazi attack reached a climax on September 16 when US Ambassador to the United Nations Susan Rice appeared on all Sunday morning political talk shows to promote this message. She delivered the now-infamous statement, "There was a vile film that was spread on the Internet. It has nothing to do with the US government, and we find it repulsive and reprehensible. It has angered many individuals worldwide. That provoked unrest around the world, including attacks on Western facilities such as embassies and consulates. That violence is inexcusable. When it comes to such a video, it is never acceptable to respond in this manner. And we've been working directly and effectively with governments in the region and around the world to protect our workers, our embassy, and condemn the violent response to this video."

Ambassador Rice's words highlight the administration's arrogance in deception. Her performances on the well watched Sunday talk show circuit demonstrate her complete devotion to the Internet video story at this time. The levels of government bureaucracy involved in vetting a high-level official's talking points for a Sunday political talk show circuit are extensive and detailed, with the goal of shielding decision makers from accountability when catastrophic judgments occur. In an ideal world, if Susan Rice made a mistake, someone would be glad to remedy it, but that is not how the bureaucracy is intended to work. When principled public servants attempt to diverge from the political agenda, they are silenced and threatened. The "I was just following orders" mentality and decentralized responsibilities assured that no single person bore the brunt of the administration's convoluted web of falsehoods and deception.

If the politicization of the lives of our heroic public servants and the administration's purposefully misleading facts aren't enough to make you suspect, consider this: why were the survivors of the Benghazi attacks hidden?

No one argues that there were many Americans working in Benghazi on the fateful night of the attack, but information about their number and location were purposefully kept hidden. There are so many information leaks in Washington that they were always considered into our plans when I worked for the Secret Service. It was believed that information would leak, and tiered security systems geared to handle leaks were the rule rather than the exception. However, following the Benghazi attacks on both the diplomatic mission and the CIA annex, the survivors received medical attention in Benghazi, were transferred to an airfield, transported first to Tripoli and then back to the United States, and treated at a facility at home, all while remaining hidden from the press and public.

All of this action was carried out without any information being leaked to the media, which is an act of logistical secrecy that I have never seen in my tenure with the government. Given the number of persons engaged in all phases of the disaster, it's incredible that no information about the survivors has leaked. Keeping a secret in the federal government is extremely difficult since information trafficking, both classified and unclassified, is a lucrative business in Washington. During my candidacy for the US Senate and my time as an agent, I was astounded by the sheer number of people wanting to break a story. Everyone wants to be part of the "information in-crowd," and there is an insatiable hunger for inside knowledge from journalists, bloggers, and unscrupulous bureaucrats looking for a detail to use as political ransom. The concern is not whether information will leak, but when.

Even in this atmosphere, time passed, and a dense veil of mystery hung over the whereabouts and condition of the Benghazi survivors. I was astounded at the intricate amount of detail involved in keeping the whereabouts of the Benghazi survivors a secret, and the preventative measures put in place to deter anyone who knew about the situation from coming out. Even now, nearly a year after the incident, CNN has reported on an unprecedented internal effort to muzzle CIA agents with knowledge of the Benghazi affair.**

Representatives Frank Wolf and Jim Gerlach wrote to Secretary of State John Kerry on March 1, 2013, citing a "reliable source" who stated that there could be up to thirty survivors of the attack, many of whom were receiving treatment at Walter Reed National Military Medical Center. If this was the case, the attempt to suppress the survivors was much more extraordinary. Something has been exchanged for their collaboration, which must be significant. Only after relentless congressional, public, and media pressure were Gregory Hicks, deputy chief of mission in Tripoli, and Mark Thompson, deputy coordinator for operations for the State Department's counterterrorism bureau, located and authorized to testify before Congress about the numerous failures that led to the deaths of our personnel in Benghazi and the tragic cover-up that followed.

However, those who worked overtime to suppress the Benghazi survivors' stories of the incident will most likely face a serious political cost. Every political expert will tell you that putting a human face on an issue makes it far more personal. The Benghazi survivors will eventually recount, in tragic detail, the events of September 11, 2012; their fear, shock, and disappointment at the complete lack of any significant US military or diplomatic response to an attack that lasted more than eight hours; and their rage at becoming pawns in the administration's cover-up.

Tears tell a tale that words can never fully convey, and those involved in the deliberate suppression of information are well aware of this fact. A word of caution to the administration: as time goes, secrets become less secret, threats become less dangerous, and promises become less rewarding. This knowledge will eventually seep out, and it has already begun to do so. Every detail of the survivors' stories of the attack will reopen a gaping wound and undermine any remaining sense of credibility for this administration. The bureaucracy is an imperfect shield that can only protect the government and its surrogates for a limited time.

Chapter 22: BOSTON: TOO MANY AGENCIES, NOT ENOUGH COMMUNICATION

The April 15, 2013, terrorist assaults in Boston marked a new chapter in our continuous fight against terrorism. In a society that attributes its success and wealth to both economic and political liberty, which we provide to everyone inside our borders, it is a pity that those who have benefited from these liberties continue to target America. Terrorists who continue to target us believe in an ideology that is diametrically opposed to freedom. Their worldview is blame-based, with the objective of achieving worldwide hegemony and forced subservience. They achieve these heinous goals by terror, death, and destruction. This isn't about religion. If this were a religious issue, the three million Muslims who currently live quietly in the United States would protest in large numbers. Rather, it is about a group of killers attempting to hijack and hide behind religion to legitimize their horrible plans.

The Obama administration's clear discomfort with openly addressing terrorism stems from the president's ideological beliefs, which lean to the far left. The Democratic Party's radical left wing is led by Democrats who believe that society can be perfect, that evil is just the result of a societal collapse, and that the United States' past faults are to blame for our current global issues. This type of foolishness is putting the American people at risk as Washington ignores the warning signs of international and domestic terrorism in an attempt to evade blame.

Having spent many years behind the scenes as a federal agent, I can witness the negative impact that a dangerously misinformed worldview can have on the rank-and-file federal investigators who work tirelessly to prevent terrorist strikes. Agents with the greatest of intentions may be blocked from pursuing an investigation due to pressure to demonstrate that their goals are solely law enforcement-related and that no judgment has been made based on the subject's religion or looks. This is specific to investigations into terror cases involving extreme Islam and adds an unneeded layer of inspection based on the notion that the excellent men and women investigating these cases would open a case based on a personal bias. This unwarranted, top-down politicization of an already closely watched government investigative process has real-world effects. Staffers who work in the insulated, crystal kingdom of Washington, DC frequently fail to comprehend the obstacles that agents face on a daily basis. This is another example of the negative repercussions that growing bureaucracy has on government employees who are merely trying to do their jobs.

The Boston Marathon bombing was unprecedented in a number of tragic aspects, and I believe it will forever alter the domestic security picture, potentially changing the perilous course we are now on.

Terrorist attacks perpetrated by Chechens are uncommon in the West. For strategic reasons, the Chechen separatist movement, which seeks autonomy for Chechnya from the Russian Federation, has avoided targeting the West, particularly the United States. The Chechens have historically considered us as geopolitical opponents of Russia, and they have avoided attacking us to avoid pulling us into their regional conflict on the Russian side. Giving the US a reason to side with Russia and coalesce around a common cause would be a tactical disaster for the separatist movement. The classic adage "the enemy of my enemy is my friend" applies to Chechen perceptions of the United States.

However, this terrorist act was not carried out by Chechen separatists, who are notorious for their brutality in attacks on Russians. It was planned and carried out by two brothers of Chechen heritage who fled their nation and settled in Boston, attending local schools, engaging in social and athletic events, and, in the older brother's case, marrying an American woman.

The Tsarnaev brothers took advantage of the compassionate clause in American immigration law for political refugees seeking asylum, and the generosity of the American social support net, to fund an attack on the country that provided them with a better life. Photos of older brother Tamerlan in dazzling clothes, and rumors about him cruising around his neighborhood in luxury cars, are glaring examples of ideological dishonesty. This ideological divide has serious implications for intelligence gathering since, in an affluent society like ours, young individuals dressed in flashy clothes and driving expensive cars are the exception rather than the norm. These two brothers were living in a typical middle-class American neighborhood. If they had suddenly abandoned all of their material luxuries to wage a twisted intellectual war against our political and economic liberties, they would have provoked a higher level of public mistrust. However, the Tsarnaev brothers presented a "normal" image to their neighbors and friends. They do not represent the usual face of terror, which made the situation even more startling.

Although large athletic events in the United States have long been sought after by international terrorist groups, no international group or individual has ever successfully carried out a terrorist plot at one. Eric Rudolph, a US citizen, carried out the 1996 Olympic Park bombing in Atlanta, which killed one and injured over 100 people. And, most importantly, with only small weapons, smokeless powder, homemade shrapnel, and two pressure cookers, an adolescent and a twentysomething were able to effectively shut down a major US metropolis for nearly an entire business week and scare its entire population.

The Boston Marathon bombing was the first successful attack on American territory in which surveillance camera technology and the controversial expansion of its deployment directly contributed to the terrorists' capture before they could do further devastation. As an increasing number of Americans feel dissatisfied with the new "surveillance society," the ongoing national debate about the trade-offs between liberty and security will undoubtedly advance.

If there was a "new normal" after the terrorist attacks of September 11, 2001, I feel we are now in a "new new normal" following the April 15, 2013, Boston incident. Despite political pronouncements to the contrary, global terrorist organizations are not "on the run"; rather, they are devising new operational models to supply their product, terror.

Although the Boston attack resulted in fewer lives and material damage than 9/11, the long-term ramifications could be substantially worse. The September 11 attacks followed a "franchise" model of terrorism in which groups of individuals, akin to franchisees in the commercial world, received training and advice from an umbrella organization yet carried out the destructive plot themselves. This contrasts with the Boston incident, in which the Tsarnaev brothers appeared to be unskilled and unsupported following the bombing. It is apparent that someone taught them how to construct the bombs, but the fact that they did not attempt to flee after the attack and carried it out without disguise demonstrates a lack of support from a bigger terrorist organization.

The sad tactical success of the Boston attack has revealed to the world the possibility of a new, more lethal type of terrorism. I call it "sole proprietorship" terrorism.

Using the increasing rise of online video sharing and social media, terrorist umbrella groups can launch the "self-radicalization" process through online jihadist propaganda and provide guidance and training through instructional content without having to get their hands dirty. Following a successful attack, the umbrella group can use the occasion to pitch new recruits.

This model poses a greater risk because self-radicalized members (or small groups, in the case of the Tsarnaevs) have few incriminating links and will leave fewer investigative and intelligence clues about the planning and operational stages of their attacks, making them more difficult to detect and prevent. The tendency toward the enlargement of the already fragmented federal law-enforcement agency complicates matters. Sole proprietorship terrorism, by definition, does not involve the networks of individuals on which the franchise model is based, and therefore reduces the likelihood that these terrorists will be identified.

My experience at the Melville field office while working on a bank fraud investigation exemplifies the divergence among federal authorities. Although the investigation was initially referred to the Secret Service as a bank fraud case, as it progressed and my target's network of contacts emerged, it became apparent that individuals of his network were the targets of other agencies' antiterrorism investigations. This relationship was discovered by chance, not due to interagency operability.

The scenario necessitated that I contact the appropriate agencies and collaborate to advance the investigation and apprehend the individuals. The cooperation was excessively difficult at times due to bureaucratic clashes, but we eventually completed our task. When there is no network or cell, or when the group is small and isolated and connects to the wider network via cyberspace, the trail of investigative warning indicators disappears. As leads grow increasingly difficult to pursue and interagency contact and information sharing get more difficult and stressful, the fragmented character of the investigative bodies can cause a sole proprietor terrorist never being caught at all, as we witnessed in Boston.

A sole proprietor may make fewer interactions that are of investigative interest than larger franchise cells, which produce far more chatter. If any of these few opportunities are missed, the chances of preventing an attack are reduced. Of course, information sharing among agencies would be superfluous if there weren't so many distinct federal law enforcement agencies operating independently and adding to the rising bureaucratic fog. The explosive growth of interagency segmentation and bureaucratic layering within agencies, combined with the growing possibility of sole-proprietor terrorism and limited investigative breadcrumbs left on the trail, are significant impediments to government counterterrorism initiatives.

We saw this similar pattern play out in the aftermath of the Boston incident, as data regarding missing investigation clues concerning the attackers surfaced. Again, these missed signs were caused by a dysfunctional and too bureaucratic, multifaceted federal law enforcement apparatus rather than a lack of dedication and mission focus on the part of the individual federal agents involved.

The way the system now works is that each agency exists solely to protect its own territory, and the multiple layers within the agencies exist to protect the layer above, distributing responsibility so that no one is truly accountable for the outcome of the game. The Boston Marathon case reminds me of the fraud investigation I led during my brief time at the Baltimore field office. We discovered a number of co-conspirators within the target's network, which I would expose as the inquiry advanced. When I submitted a suspect into the Secret Service's archaic database and another Secret Service agent expressed interest in that subject, a message appeared with the agent's phone number and case number. As is typical investigative technique, I checked into the investigating agent's case for background information using the same approach and then followed up with a detailed phone conversation to make the connections and piece together the investigative puzzle.

If the data-sharing method I described seemed straightforward, it is because it was. Even using an old system, such as that used by the Secret Service at the time, agents were able to locate the information and connections needed to advance the investigation. Compare this antiquated, underfunded system to the multibillion-dollar probe into

Tamerlan Tsarnaev's radicalization by current federal authorities. His name was recorded into a number of databases, including the FBI's Guardian Database, the Terrorist Identities Datamart Environment (TIDES), the Terrorist Screening Database (TSDB), and the Treasury Enforcement Communication System (TECS), which is run by US Customs and Border Protection. Even after searching all these advanced data platforms, federal law enforcement was unable to provide any valuable interagency investigative communication, resulting in the loss of innocent American lives.

Following the Boston Marathon assault, we discovered that the Russian FSB (the former KGB) had already informed the FBI of Tamerlan's possible radicalization in March 2011. The FBI conducted a preliminary inquiry that produced no significant results and finished in June 2011. In September 2011, the Russian FSB warned the CIA about Tamerlan's alleged radical affiliations. Tamerlan traveled to Russia in January 2012, triggering an alert in the TECS database, and when he returned to Boston in July 2012, another TECS alert was initiated.

Why weren't the alarms followed? The answer is straightforward: too many agencies, databases, and competing agendas. The expansion of bureaucracy at the expense of field agents who are laser-focused on counterterrorism only serves to distribute responsibility among the bureaucratic layers, none of which are incentivized to produce an answer and be held accountable for the American lives lost and traumatized by a terror attack.

The American people must demand serious solutions to this situation. Having worked within this bureaucratic fog, I am constantly perplexed as to why no one is seriously proposing an obvious solution to these problems: a streamlined, decompartmentalized federal law-enforcement organization under one umbrella, with one person at the helm responsible for its mission.

This umbrella organization could be organized by various law-enforcement specialties (financial crimes, drug enforcement, counterterrorism, diplomatic protection, etc.). Communication and information sharing issues between agencies would be replaced by far less serious intra-agency squabbles that are easier to resolve. Databases might be combined under a single organization, and access to them improved and expanded. Eliminating redundant assignments would allow staff to be reassigned based on national priorities. The suffocating layers of management would be removed, and rigorous accountability chains established. Office space could be reduced, and equipment and sophisticated law-enforcement laboratories could be combined for "one-stop shopping." Thousands of duplicative federal administrative forms that achieve the same goal via redundant agency administrative paths would be eliminated, ushering in a new era of accountability.

Along with a major overhaul of our federal law enforcement agency, I believe new security models must evolve. The threat of terrorism is unlikely to go away anytime soon, despite the present administration's assumption that evil is only the result of social shortcomings. I would argue that humanity's vast history contradicts that premise. Violence has always been about a raw display of power, and there are far too many motivations for people to engage in it. Violence has a terrible but very real power for someone who feels disenfranchised or who has not received the money power, status, and societal acceptability that come with success. When society has abandoned you, for whatever reason, whether owing to your own failures or events beyond your control, you will seek purpose in what has become a meaningless life. That meaning could stem from group acceptance of a gang, personal strength via violence at the expense of others, or a warped ideological platform that explains your own faults. Jihadist propaganda, widely available in a world made smaller by the expansion of Internet communication, will serve as a platform for an increasing number of the world's Tsarnaev brothers seeking a cause and a means of making their voice to the world.

It comes as no surprise to the intelligence or law enforcement communities that jihadist propaganda would appeal to a segment of our society, and that self-radicalization is not only feasible, but quite likely for some of our own citizens. The hardships of daily American life, and our obligations to our families and employment, provide order and structure to our lives, eliminating the need to engage in violent propaganda. We tend to see the world as a series of actions and consequences, and the concept of using fatal force to advance a cause is repellent to the majority of us. However, violence to attain an ideological goal, no matter how repugnant to civilized men and women, has been the norm for the majority of human history. The ability to use force to enslave those you consider adversaries or to steal what you want, whether earned or not, is pretty natural, and the power gained can promote that type of behavior. Our extraordinary degree of riches, along with the fulfillment of the majority of our basic human needs, makes the concept of "violence as natural" so strange to us.

This poses an obvious risk to a society seeking to prevent terrorists from causing the widespread devastation they inflicted in Boston. Once again, the franchise model of terrorism necessitates interaction, and each engagement generates a ripple that, if identified, can be utilized to investigate and prevent an attack. One person working alone causes less ripples and has a much better chance of escaping notice. Unfortunately, this will certainly cause a new set of security measures and restrictions on individual liberties that we are not used to in the United States. These encroachments will not be voluntary, and they will undoubtedly alter how we perceive public events in the future. Subjecting yourself to a pat down at a public event may become regular operating practice, and security cameras will expand to the point where any public space in a big city will most likely be monitored.

The New Year's Eve celebration in Times Square and the presidential inauguration are two high-profile outdoor events with enormous audiences that have effectively implemented security arrangements that have kept all participants safe so far. The security models utilized by the New York City Police Department and the Secret Service for these events are likely to become the standard in the future. These events draw millions of people, and despite some hiccups, they have never experienced a major security compromise. Security officials do this by designating "access zones" where the public can watch the event. These models, like the "box within a box" approach I discussed previously in the book, do not try the impossible.

During several interviews I gave prior to the 2012 presidential inauguration, I was asked, "How does the Secret Service secure the entire city for the inauguration?""The answer is that they don't. The same technique is employed in Washington as it was for President Obama's Caterpillar manufacturing tour, which I coordinated. The facility was full with dangerous equipment and chemicals, so we created a "box" within it and concentrated our limited resources on securing that small region. The DC Metro police and other law enforcement organizations can secure Washington's streets, but the Secret Service PPD is solely responsible for securing the president's location. During the inauguration, we accomplished this by strategically placing barriers to ensure that persons who accessed areas near the president did so only through certain "people-funnel" checks.

We insist on everyone passing through a metal detector at presidential inaugurations, but this is not required to significantly minimize the chance of another Boston-style incident. The Boston bombers used antipersonnel improvised explosive devices (IEDs) intended to murder or maim a significant number of people while instilling fear. That type of attack requires a large crowd in which to detonate the bomb. If the Boston Police Department had implemented a marathon plan similar to the NYPD's Times Square plan, in which anyone entering areas such as the starting line, halfway point, and finish line, where people tend to congregate, was subjected to a bag check and quick pat-down in lieu of metal detectors, the attackers would have had to reconsider their strategy.

It bothers me to have to propose a "new normal" way of living in our country because of the loss of individual liberty that would occur due to heightened security. So far, lawmakers have made no progress in updating legislation that safeguards individual liberties and the right to privacy. Provisions in poorly drafted provisions of the PATRIOT Act, for example, have been abused and will continue to be so unless the law is improved. Furthermore, the billions of money spent on federalizing airport security have continuously failed to yield the anticipated results, subjecting the people to inconvenient, frequently embarrassing security screenings.

The trend toward a surveillance state teaches us that no security measure is without a trade-off. According to Israeli major general and terror specialist Amos Yadlin, "it's not the tools but the rules of engagement." The PATRIOT Act was a tool with poorly defined rules of engagement that were subject to interpretation by law enforcement officials. When the regulations are open to interpretation, law enforcement will always seek the broadest possible meaning to support their case. It is not personal; the men and women in federal law enforcement with whom I have worked are members of our larger communities—fathers, moms, neighbors, soccer coaches—and have no personal motivation to violate your rights. They are merely dealing with a collection of imperfect tools.

The same can be said about increasing the use of security cameras. Surveillance cameras are not necessarily evil, but when government officials are uncertain about the rules of engagement, such as where these cameras will be placed, why they will be placed, and what will be done with the footage, Americans understandably become concerned. Surveillance, in my experience, is only nonthreatening to those who are observing, not those being watched.

128

Chapter 23: OUR GOVERNMENT HAS FAILED US

The April 15, 2013, terrorist assaults in Boston marked a new chapter in our continuous fight against terrorism. In a society that attributes its success and wealth to both economic and political liberty, which we provide to everyone inside our borders, it is a pity that those who have benefited from these liberties continue to target America. Terrorists who continue to target us believe in an ideology that is diametrically opposed to freedom. Their worldview is blame-based, with the objective of achieving worldwide hegemony and forced subservience. They achieve these heinous goals by terror, death, and destruction. This isn't about religion. If this were a religious issue, the three million Muslims who currently live quietly in the United States would protest in large numbers. Rather, it is about a group of killers attempting to hijack and hide behind religion to legitimize their horrible plans.

The Obama administration's clear discomfort with openly addressing terrorism stems from the president's ideological beliefs, which lean to the far left. The Democratic Party's radical left wing is led by Democrats who believe that society can be perfect, that evil is just the result of a societal collapse, and that the United States' past faults are to blame for our current global issues. This type of foolishness is putting the American people at risk as Washington ignores the warning signs of international and domestic terrorism in an attempt to evade blame.

Having spent many years behind the scenes as a federal agent, I can witness the negative impact that a dangerously misinformed worldview can have on the rank-and-file federal investigators who work tirelessly to prevent terrorist strikes. Agents with the greatest of intentions may be blocked from pursuing an investigation due to pressure to demonstrate that their goals are solely law enforcement-related and that no judgment has been made based on the subject's religion or looks. This is specific to investigations into terror cases involving extreme Islam and adds an unneeded layer of inspection based on the notion that the excellent men and women investigating these cases would open a case based on a personal bias. This unwarranted, top-down politicization of an already closely watched government investigative process has real-world effects. Staffers who work in the insulated, crystal kingdom of Washington, DC frequently fail to comprehend the obstacles that agents face on a daily basis. This is another example of the negative repercussions that growing bureaucracy has on government employees who are merely trying to do their jobs.

The Boston Marathon bombing was unprecedented in a number of tragic aspects, and I believe it will forever alter the domestic security picture, potentially changing the perilous course we are now on.

Terrorist attacks perpetrated by Chechens are uncommon in the West. For strategic reasons, the Chechen separatist movement, which seeks autonomy for Chechnya from the Russian Federation, has avoided targeting the West, particularly the United States. The Chechens have historically considered us as geopolitical opponents of Russia, and they have avoided attacking us to avoid pulling us into their regional conflict on the Russian side. Giving the US a reason to side with Russia and coalesce around a common cause would be a tactical disaster for the separatist movement. The classic adage "the enemy of my enemy is my friend" applies to Chechen perceptions of the United States.

However, this terrorist act was not carried out by Chechen separatists, who are notorious for their brutality in attacks on Russians. It was planned and carried out by two brothers of Chechen heritage who fled their nation and settled in Boston, attending local schools, engaging in social and athletic events, and, in the older brother's case, marrying an American woman.

The Tsarnaev brothers took advantage of the compassionate clause in American immigration law for political refugees seeking asylum, and the generosity of the American social support net, to fund an attack on the country that provided them with a better life. Photos of older brother Tamerlan in dazzling clothes, and rumors about him cruising around his neighborhood in luxury cars, are glaring examples of ideological dishonesty. This ideological divide has serious implications for intelligence gathering since, in an affluent society like ours, young individuals dressed in flashy clothes and driving expensive cars are the exception rather than the norm. These two brothers were living in a typical middle-class American neighborhood. If they had suddenly abandoned all of their material luxuries to wage a twisted intellectual war against our political and economic liberties, they would have provoked a higher level of public mistrust. However, the Tsarnaev brothers presented a "normal" image to their neighbors and friends. They do not represent the usual face of terror, which made the situation even more startling.

Although large athletic events in the United States have long been sought after by international terrorist groups, no international group or individual has ever successfully carried out a terrorist plot at one. Eric Rudolph, a US citizen, carried out the 1996 Olympic Park bombing in Atlanta, which killed one and injured over 100 people. And, most importantly, with only small weapons, smokeless powder, homemade shrapnel, and two pressure cookers, an adolescent and a twentysomething were able to effectively shut down a major US metropolis for nearly an entire business week and scare its entire population.

The Boston Marathon bombing was the first successful attack on American territory in which surveillance camera technology and the controversial expansion of its deployment directly contributed to the terrorists' capture before they could do further devastation. As an increasing number of Americans feel dissatisfied with the new "surveillance society," the ongoing national debate about the trade-offs between liberty and security will undoubtedly advance.

If there was a "new normal" after the terrorist attacks of September 11, 2001, I feel we are now in a "new new normal" following the April 15, 2013, Boston incident. Despite political pronouncements to the contrary, global terrorist organizations are not "on the run"; rather, they are devising new operational models to supply their product, terror.

Although the Boston attack resulted in fewer lives and material damage than 9/11, the long-term ramifications could be substantially worse. The September 11 attacks followed a "franchise" model of terrorism in which groups of individuals, akin to franchisees in the commercial world, received training and advice from an umbrella organization yet carried out the destructive plot themselves. This contrasts with the Boston incident, in which the Tsarnaev brothers appeared to be unskilled and unsupported following the bombing. It is apparent that someone taught them how to construct the bombs, but the fact that they did not attempt to flee after the attack and carried it out without disguise demonstrates a lack of support from a bigger terrorist organization.

The sad tactical success of the Boston attack has revealed to the world the possibility of a new, more lethal type of terrorism. I call it "sole proprietorship" terrorism.

Using the increasing rise of online video sharing and social media, terrorist umbrella groups can launch the "self-radicalization" process through online jihadist propaganda and provide guidance and training through instructional content without having to get their hands dirty. Following a successful attack, the umbrella group can use the occasion to pitch new recruits.

This model poses a greater risk because self-radicalized members (or small groups, in the case of the Tsarnaevs) have few incriminating links and will leave fewer investigative and intelligence clues about the planning and operational stages of their attacks, making them more difficult to detect and prevent. The tendency toward the enlargement of the already fragmented federal law-enforcement agency complicates matters. Sole proprietorship terrorism, by definition, does not involve the networks of individuals on which the franchise model is based, and therefore reduces the likelihood that these terrorists will be identified.

My experience at the Melville field office while working on a bank fraud investigation exemplifies the divergence among federal authorities. Although the investigation was initially referred to the Secret Service as a bank fraud case, as it progressed and my target's network of contacts emerged, it became apparent that individuals of his network were the targets of other agencies' antiterrorism investigations. This relationship was discovered by chance, not due to interagency operability.

The scenario necessitated that I contact the appropriate agencies and collaborate to advance the investigation and apprehend the individuals. The cooperation was excessively difficult at times due to bureaucratic clashes, but we eventually completed our task. When there is no network or cell, or when the group is small and isolated and connects to the wider network via cyberspace, the trail of investigative warning indicators disappears. As leads grow increasingly difficult to pursue and interagency contact and information sharing get more difficult and stressful, the fragmented character of the investigative bodies can cause a sole proprietor terrorist never being caught at all, as we witnessed in Boston.

A sole proprietor may make fewer interactions that are of investigative interest than larger franchise cells, which produce far more chatter. If any of these few opportunities are missed, the chances of preventing an attack are reduced. Of course, information sharing among agencies would be superfluous if there weren't so many distinct federal law enforcement agencies operating independently and adding to the rising bureaucratic fog. The explosive growth of interagency segmentation and bureaucratic layering within agencies, combined with the growing possibility of sole-proprietor terrorism and limited investigative breadcrumbs left on the trail, are significant impediments to government counterterrorism initiatives.

We saw this similar pattern play out in the aftermath of the Boston incident, as data regarding missing investigation clues concerning the attackers surfaced. Again, these missed signs were caused by a dysfunctional and too bureaucratic, multifaceted federal law enforcement apparatus rather than a lack of dedication and mission focus on the part of the individual federal agents involved.

The way the system now works is that each agency exists solely to protect its own territory, and the multiple layers within the agencies exist to protect the layer above, distributing responsibility so that no one is truly accountable for the outcome of the game. The Boston Marathon case reminds me of the fraud investigation I led during my brief time at the Baltimore field office. We discovered a number of co-conspirators within the target's network, which I would expose as the inquiry advanced. When I submitted a suspect into the Secret Service's archaic database and another Secret Service agent expressed interest in that subject, a message appeared with the agent's phone number and case number. As is typical investigative technique, I checked into the investigating agent's case for background information using the same approach and then followed up with a detailed phone conversation to make the connections and piece together the investigative puzzle.

If the data-sharing method I described seemed straightforward, it is because it was. Even using an old system, such as that used by the Secret Service at the time, agents were able to locate the information and connections needed to advance the investigation. Compare this antiquated, underfunded system to the multibillion-dollar probe into

Tamerlan Tsarnaev's radicalization by current federal authorities. His name was recorded into a number of databases, including the FBI's Guardian Database, the Terrorist Identities Datamart Environment (TIDES), the Terrorist Screening Database (TSDB), and the Treasury Enforcement Communication System (TECS), which is run by US Customs and Border Protection. Even after searching all these advanced data platforms, federal law enforcement was unable to provide any valuable interagency investigative communication, resulting in the loss of innocent American lives.

Following the Boston Marathon assault, we discovered that the Russian FSB (the former KGB) had already informed the FBI of Tamerlan's possible radicalization in March 2011. The FBI conducted a preliminary inquiry that produced no significant results and finished in June 2011. In September 2011, the Russian FSB warned the CIA about Tamerlan's alleged radical affiliations. Tamerlan traveled to Russia in January 2012, triggering an alert in the TECS database, and when he returned to Boston in July 2012, another TECS alert was initiated.

Why weren't the alarms followed? The answer is straightforward: too many agencies, databases, and competing agendas. The expansion of bureaucracy at the expense of field agents who are laser-focused on counterterrorism only serves to distribute responsibility among the bureaucratic layers, none of which are incentivized to produce an answer and be held accountable for the American lives lost and traumatized by a terror attack.

The American people must demand serious solutions to this situation. Having worked within this bureaucratic fog, I am constantly perplexed as to why no one is seriously proposing an obvious solution to these problems: a streamlined, decompartmentalized federal law-enforcement organization under one umbrella, with one person at the helm responsible for its mission.

This umbrella organization could be organized by various law-enforcement specialties (financial crimes, drug enforcement, counterterrorism, diplomatic protection, etc.). Communication and information sharing issues between agencies would be replaced by far less serious intra-agency squabbles that are easier to resolve. Databases might be combined under a single organization, and access to them improved and expanded. Eliminating redundant assignments would allow staff to be reassigned based on national priorities. The suffocating layers of management would be removed, and rigorous accountability chains established. Office space could be reduced, and equipment and sophisticated law-enforcement laboratories could be combined for "one-stop shopping." Thousands of duplicative federal administrative forms that achieve the same goal via redundant agency administrative paths would be eliminated, ushering in a new era of accountability.

Along with a major overhaul of our federal law enforcement agency, I believe new security models must evolve. The threat of terrorism is unlikely to go away anytime soon, despite the present administration's assumption that evil is only the result of social shortcomings. I would argue that humanity's vast history contradicts that premise. Violence has always been about a raw display of power, and there are far too many motivations for people to engage in it. Violence has a terrible but very real power for someone who feels disenfranchised or who has not received the money power, status, and societal acceptability that come with success. When society has abandoned you, for whatever reason, whether owing to your own failures or events beyond your control, you will seek purpose in what has become a meaningless life. That meaning could stem from group acceptance of a gang, personal strength via violence at the expense of others, or a warped ideological platform that explains your own faults. Jihadist propaganda, widely available in a world made smaller by the expansion of Internet communication, will serve as a platform for an increasing number of the world's Tsarnaev brothers seeking a cause and a means of making their voice to the world.

It comes as no surprise to the intelligence or law enforcement communities that jihadist propaganda would appeal to a segment of our society, and that self-radicalization is not only feasible, but quite likely for some of our own citizens. The hardships of daily American life, and our obligations to our families and employment, provide order and structure to our lives, eliminating the need to engage in violent propaganda. We tend to see the world as a series of actions and consequences, and the concept of using fatal force to advance a cause is repellent to the majority of us. However, violence to attain an ideological goal, no matter how repugnant to civilized men and women, has been the norm for the majority of human history. The ability to use force to enslave those you consider adversaries or to steal what you want, whether earned or not, is pretty natural, and the power gained can promote that type of behavior. Our extraordinary degree of riches, along with the fulfillment of the majority of our basic human needs, makes the concept of "violence as natural" so strange to us.

This poses an obvious risk to a society seeking to prevent terrorists from causing the widespread devastation they inflicted in Boston. Once again, the franchise model of terrorism necessitates interaction, and each engagement generates a ripple that, if identified, can be utilized to investigate and prevent an attack. One person working alone causes less ripples and has a much better chance of escaping notice. Unfortunately, this will certainly cause a new set of security measures and restrictions on individual liberties that we are not used to in the United States. These encroachments will not be voluntary, and they will undoubtedly alter how we perceive public events in the future. Subjecting yourself to a pat down at a public event may become regular operating practice, and security cameras will expand to the point where any public space in a big city will most likely be monitored.

The New Year's Eve celebration in Times Square and the presidential inauguration are two high-profile outdoor events with enormous audiences that have effectively implemented security arrangements that have kept all participants safe so far. The security models utilized by the New York City Police Department and the Secret Service for these events are likely to become the standard in the future. These events draw millions of people, and despite some hiccups, they have never experienced a major security compromise. Security officials do this by designating "access zones" where the public can watch the event. These models, like the "box within a box" approach I discussed previously in the book, do not try the impossible.

During several interviews I gave prior to the 2012 presidential inauguration, I was asked, "How does the Secret Service secure the entire city for the inauguration?""The answer is that they don't. The same technique is employed in Washington as it was for President Obama's Caterpillar manufacturing tour, which I coordinated. The facility was full with dangerous equipment and chemicals, so we created a "box" within it and concentrated our limited resources on securing that small region. The DC Metro police and other law enforcement organizations can secure Washington's streets, but the Secret Service PPD is solely responsible for securing the president's location. During the inauguration, we accomplished this by strategically placing barriers to ensure that persons who accessed areas near the president did so only through certain "people-funnel" checks.

We insist on everyone passing through a metal detector at presidential inaugurations, but this is not required to significantly minimize the chance of another Boston-style incident. The Boston bombers used antipersonnel improvised explosive devices (IEDs) intended to murder or maim a significant number of people while instilling fear. That type of attack requires a large crowd in which to detonate the bomb. If the Boston Police Department had implemented a marathon plan similar to the NYPD's Times Square plan, in which anyone entering areas such as the starting line, halfway point, and finish line, where people tend to congregate, was subjected to a bag check and quick pat-down in lieu of metal detectors, the attackers would have had to reconsider their strategy.

It bothers me to have to propose a "new normal" way of living in our country because of the loss of individual liberty that would occur due to heightened security. So far, lawmakers have made no progress in updating legislation that safeguards individual liberties and the right to privacy. Provisions in poorly drafted provisions of the PATRIOT Act, for example, have been abused and will continue to be so unless the law is improved. Furthermore, the billions of money spent on federalizing airport security have continuously failed to yield the anticipated results, subjecting the people to inconvenient, frequently embarrassing security screenings.

The trend toward a surveillance state teaches us that no security measure is without a trade-off. According to Israeli major general and terror specialist Amos Yadlin, "it's not the tools but the rules of engagement." The PATRIOT Act was a tool with poorly defined rules of engagement that were subject to interpretation by law enforcement officials. When the regulations are open to interpretation, law enforcement will always seek the broadest possible meaning to support their case. It is not personal; the men and women in federal law enforcement with whom I have worked are members of our larger communities—fathers, moms, neighbors, soccer coaches—and have no personal motivation to violate your rights. They are merely dealing with a collection of imperfect tools.

The same can be said about increasing the use of security cameras. Surveillance cameras are not necessarily evil, but when government officials are uncertain about the rules of engagement, such as where these cameras will be placed, why they will be placed, and what will be done with the footage, Americans understandably become concerned. Surveillance, in my experience, is only nonthreatening to those who are observing, not those being watched.

Copyright © 2024

All rights reserved

The content of this book may not be reproduced, duplicated, or transmitted without the author's or publisher's express written permission. Under no circumstances will the publisher or author be held liable or legally responsible for any damages, reparation, or monetary loss caused by the information contained in this book, whether directly or indirectly.

Legal Notice:

This publication is copyrighted. It is strictly for personal use only. You may not change, distribute, sell, use, quote, or paraphrase any part of this book without the author's or publisher's permission.

Disclaimer Notice:

Please note that the information in this document is for educational and entertainment purposes. Every effort has been made to present accurate, up-to-date, reliable, and comprehensive information. There are no express or implied warranties. Readers understand that the author is not providing legal, financial, medical, or professional advice. This book's content was compiled from a variety of sources. Please seek the advice of a licensed professional before attempting any of the techniques described in this book. By reading this document, the reader agrees that the author is not liable for any direct or indirect losses incurred due to using the information contained within this document, including, but not limited to, errors, omissions, or inaccuracies.

Printed in Great Britain
by Amazon